I STILL OWN
A FLIP PHONE
And I Wear Skinny Jeans

By

Mike Turnbull

All photos were taken by Mike
Turnbull, using his flip phone, except
the pictures appearing on pages 87–89.

ISBN-13:
ISBN-10:
First published in 2017

DEDICATION

This book is dedicated to anyone who has ever been picked on or ridiculed for their seeming lack of mastery of technology. I want all of you to know you will be okay. Some of us choose to keep it simple. I don't do Facebook, I do not have a Twitter account, but I have no idea how to Snapchat. If I could go completely off the grid, I would. I haven't quite figured out how to do that, but I will work on it in retirement. I know there are more flip phone users out there; hopefully we will meet up sometime.

PREFACE

I am 56 years old and I have owned three cell phones in my lifetime. All three of these, including my current phone, have been flip phones.

My first phone wore out, and I dropped my second phone in the lake two summers ago. It is somewhere at the bottom of Fall Lake in about twenty-five feet of water, so I am confident my contacts are safe.

It was very difficult to get the second phone replaced with another flip phone. The girl at the AT&T store had a tough time finding one in the storage room. She tried everything to talk me into buying a smart phone, but I didn't bite.

I told her that all I needed the phone to do was send and receive phone calls. If it could take pictures, that was a bonus. She said texting was part of the service. I told her that I read and deleted texted messages but rarely send one myself. She was dismayed, but informed me that texting had to be provided even if I don't make extensive use of it. I don't need the internet or email capability on my phone, so she eliminated those.

There are several perks to owning a flip phone, including:

1] I can leave my phone anywhere; nobody wants to steal it. Most kids don't even know what it is.

2] Inexpensive service contract.

3] My student-athletes get a kick out of it.

4] My own kids are instantly embarrassed when I use it in public. (It's always fun to embarrass your own children.)

5] On very rare occasions I run into another flip phone owner and it always makes for candid conversation and some quality bonding time. It is like an underground support group.

6] Teenage kids just stare at it and occasionally ask what it is. I never pass on an opportunity to educate the youth.

7] I am never rude in public by breaking out my phone and scrolling through it, clearing texts, checking email, or searching the internet.

8] I never have an awkward argument with Siiri or Google.

9] I seem to be the smartest person in the room when I answer a trivia question without Googling it on my phone.

10] I never have to show people pictures because they are too small.

11] I don't have to worry about purchasing Apps or searching for free ones.

12] Occasionally I receive validation when I learn of someone famous using a flip phone (most recently Jerry Jones — Dallas Cowboy owner — and Andrew Luck — Indianapolis Colt quarterback).

I have only experienced a few drawbacks and difficulties associated with owning a flip phone, and so far I'm doing fine.

1] If I have a picture I want to SAVED, I send it to one of my kids and ask them to send it to my computer at work.

2] I can't Facetime my grandson. (This might be the deal breaker.)

3] I need to put on glasses to see the screen.

4] Ringtones are a little sappy, but I always know it is my phone.

Other than these few minor difficulties, it is all good!

What I have decided to do is document my exchanges of texts over one year's time. I am hoping to prove that, for the most part, they are pointless and probably could have been done in a more personal and direct manner. Possibly a phone call, voicemail or — do I dare suggest it? — a face-to-face conversation.

I have already admitted that I rarely texted. I have had to cave in a little lately and texted some prospective recruits. (I coach college volleyball.) Very few of them have voicemail boxes that have been set up on their phones and they don't really keep track of email. Also, they don't answer unless they know who is calling. Texting seems to consistently get through, though. As our staff at the college gets younger, I've noticed their main means of communication is texting as well.

I have changed names and initials to protect the innocent; I do not want this book to get hacked. If this unofficial experiment fails, I will buy a smart phone. I'm also pretty sure I will not be able to purchase a fourth flip phone when the time comes anyway. I have already had a hard time moving past Eight Tracks, VCR, and cassette tapes. I recently purchased a new/used truck and had a tough time finding one with a CD player. Probably doesn't need to be said, but I cancelled the On Star immediately. The Sirius radio is free for three months, so I kept that.

I STILL OWN A FLIP PHONE
And I Wear Skinny Jeans

June 25, 2015

                         < Sent KB a picture of the
                         Testicle Festival in Nebraska

> KB: Holy shit, you texted   < TEXTED BACK: Yep!

June 28, 2015
> LB: Sent picture of my   SAVED
grandson

                         < Sent KB picture of Brau
                         Brothers

> KB: Oh boy….. you are see-   DELETED
ing all the sights!

June 29, 2015
> CV: 1109 11th St. North   < FORWARDED TO B
Apt. B

June 30, 2015
> SH: Check-in room 11:00,   DELETED
Lunch 11:30
Coaches' meeting 12:00
> SH: Team practice until   DELETED
1:45
> SH: 12:45 Check-in/Team   DELETED (Called SH)
practice until 2:15
> JJ: Thanks for the email. So   < CALLED BACK: (Left mes-
fun, Congrats!   sage) Thanks, he's great!

July 3, 2015
> RP: I will be at the Road-   < TEXTED BACK: OK
house tonite at 6:00 Celebra-
tion for everyone born in

Winton Hospital
My wife was. Stop by if you
are around.

July 7, 2015
> KB: Hey coaches… if you   < FORWARDED TO VOL-
have any female athletes in   LEYBALL PLAYERS
need of a roommate in the
dorm let me know SO needs
a roommate.

July 9, 2015
> KB: Never mind, it is S that   < TEXTED BACK: Told you!
mows the grass without a
shirt on.
> KB: No, as soon as I saw it,   < TEXTED BACK: ?????
it all made sense.
> JL: Are you in Hibbing?   < CALLED BACK
> LB: Sent picture of grand-   SAVED
son

July 10, 2015
                                   < Sent MF picture of blow-
                                   up doll at my son's bachelor
                                   party.
> MF: Your new girlfriend?   < CALLED BACK

July 19, 2015
                                   < Sent B picture of floor proj-
                                   ect at cabin
> B: Glad I missed this one!   DELETED
> KB: I fixed the website. So   < CALLED BACK &
forms should be available. I   thanked.
emailed also.
> MR: G says the course is a   DELETED
tough walk for all 18 holes.

Northland Country Club
3901 E Superior St.

July 21, 2015
> KB: Just spoke with E.   < CALLED BACK
Housing is full.

July 22, 2015
> LB: Sent picture of grand-   SAVED
son

July 23, 2015
> B: Sent scan of article in   < CALLED BACK: I couldn't
Brainerd paper   read it.

> JM: Can you come to   < CALLED BACK: I'll be
Pacesetter party on Saturday   there.
night at St. Bens. We want to
honor you and D.

July 24, 2015
> DP: Are you guys in Ely   < CALLED NUMBER: What
next weekend? This is D.   does BTW stand for?
BTW

July 25, 2015
> B: Sent picture from Wrig-   < SAVED/TEXTED BACK:
ley Field   Jealous!
> LB: Sent video of grandson   SAVED

July 27, 2015
> MF: J&J are selling football   < CALLED BACK: (Left mes-
cards for fundraiser.   sage) I'm in for $20 each.one.
> MF: Sounds good!   DELETED

July 29, 2015
> JM: Kelly Inn, you are   < TEXTED BACK: OK

3

bunking with PM

> LB: Sent picture of grand-son	SAVED
> JM: Could you go on houseboat 8/6 0r 7/10?	< CALLED BACK: (Left message) No, familyat lake and volleyball starts the 9th.

July 30, 2015

> JM: Okay maybe next spring would be better.	DELETED
> Unknown: Are you at the college? I'm in Chisholm.	DELETED

August 1, 2015

	< Sent B a picture of a sign to see if A couldmake one
> B: Yeah it would take a while.	< TEXTED BACK: OK
> B: Lots of letters.	DELETED

August 2, 2015

> MR: What year did you graduate from Ely?	< TEXTED BACK: Yes 1977?
> MR: P thought that was the year.	DELETED
> L: I see J doesn't still.	< TEXTED BACK: ?

August 3, 2015

> JM: You are probably busy. Can you be in Glencoe to-morrow to do a volleyball camp? $900/3 Days	< TEXTED BACK: No
> JM: Ok Thanks	DELETED
> C: Hey coach, sorry I was at work, my petition went through.	< TEXTED BACK: Great news!
> LR: Just leaving, hope to be there by sunset.	DELETED
	< CALLED MF: (Left mes-

> MF: She left me a message. I'm not in my office until Sunday unless it rains.
> MF: I didn't have keys for J's cage either. You'll have to call her.

sage) Anything from C?
< TEXTED BACK: ok

< CALLED BACK: I did

August 4. 2015
> TR: What is the combination to basketball storage?

< CALLED BACK (Left answer in a message.)

August 5, 2015
> JL: Can we talk?
> JL: I know you can't texted well.
> TR: What is K's number?
> TR: Sorry you shouldn't have received that.
> JJ: What do you guys pay line judges?
> JJ: Thanks

< CALLED BACK (Talked.)
DELETED

< TEXTED BACK: ?
DELETED

< TEXTED BACK: ? Call MF

DELETED

August 8, 2015
> LB: Video of grandson in the pool.

SAVED

August 9, 2015
> EG: Hey coach this is E. Since I'm so sad I can't play. I really want to be around as much as I can. If you need an extra hand with stats, let me know.
> JG: What can you return?

< CALLED BACK (Talked.)

< CALLED BACK: (Left message.) You owe $225.

August 10, 2015
> JL: Sorry Mike, did you say   < TEXTED BACK: 10:30
9:30 or 10:30?
> JL: Got it!   DELETED
> JL: I'll be in at 6:00 if any- .< TEXTED BACK: ok
one needs anything

August 11, 2015
> GM: Hey coach it's G.   SAVED number to contacts.
                                 DELETED

August 12, 2015
> AN: [218] 9**-****   SAVED number to contacts.
                                 DELETED

August 13, 2015
> LB: Picture of grandson.   SAVED

August 14, 2015
> JJ: You are all coming,   DELETED (I was already on
right?   my way.)
> MM: We play at 11:00   < TEXTED BACK: yep!
right?
> JJ: Correct, drive safe!   DELETED (Not for me.)
> UK: Yep! *UK=unknown   DELETED
> GG: When can I take pic-   DELETED (Emailed practice
tures.   schedule.)
> B: 310 State Avenue   DELETED (Had called for an
                                 address.)

August 15, 2015   FORWARDED to JL.
> RP: Fish fry this afternoon   < CALLED BACK: (Left mes-
at cabin on Fall Lake stop by!   sage) I'm not at the lake.
> JJ: L said they have a team.   < TEXTED BACK: Yay! (Had
                                 called earlier about FDL)
> JL: Got it!   DELETED
                                 < CALLED EH: (Left mes-
                                 sage) What time are you
                                 going to be here?
> EH: Pictures at 3:00,   DELETED

meeting at 2:30

August 18, 2015
> JM: Look at pacesetter.com   DELETED (I looked at it.)
if you get a chance.

August 19, 2015
> C: Can my sister come to   < TEXTED BACK: Yes
practice tomorrow?
> C: Okay, thanks!   DELETED

August 21, 2015
> E: Hey coach, let me know   DELETED
when you are scrimmaging.
I want to come and let some
stress out on some volley-
balls. Ha! Ha!
> L: Video of grandson.   SAVED
> P: Nothing there.   DELETED
> L: Didn't know that was   DELETED
sent.

Side note: Why am I included in group messages that don't
pertain to me?

August 24, 2015
> G: I know you don't re-   DELETED
spond to texts, but FYI my
work study stuff is in…
Just have to do the training
video.
> LR: CALL MOM, JUST TO   DELETED (I called my
SAY HI WHEN YOU HAVE   mom.)
5 MINUTES. Her good
friend M is in hospice soon
to die. Mom is a little down.
PLEASE DON'T TELL HER I
TOLD YOU TO CALL. SHE

DOESN'T FEEL HEARS
FROM HER FAMILY
ENOUGH. T CALLS EVERY
DAY. SHE IS THE "WON-
DERFUL" DAUGHTER.

> LK: Did my book arrive?   < CALLED BACK (It had arrived but I hadn't seen it. Read it next day and called back to congratulate her on being an author.)

> JJ: What's up?   < CALLED BACK (Talked.)

August 27, 2015
> C: Coach I've been up all night with a fever, cough and congestion. Should I stick it out and go to school, I'm not sure?   Talked face to face at practice after classes.

August 28, 2015
> JJ: We beat Northland!   < TEXTED BACK: Nice!
> JJ: How'd you do?   < TEXTED BACK: Won 25-13, 25-10, 25-8 Forwarded to K & MF
> JJ: Oh man, big scores!   < TEXTED BACK: Your score?
> JJ: 25-11, 25-22, 19-25, 26-24   DELETED (Called back.)
> KB: Your manager sent them a long time ago.   DELETED

August 29, 2015
> MF: Just got a texted from E. She is not coming today. I can't text N to see if her mom can do it. I'll let you know.   < CALLED BACK: (Left message) N's mom can't, call K.
> LB: Video of grandson.   SAVED

August 31, 2015

> G: I know you don't RE-SPOND... but a little FYI is that I have to go to K's to program my Mac. I might be late to practice and might have food in my hands.

DELETED (Read after practice.)

> TR: Good player from Ironwood. Lefty 5"10" long and athletic. Volleyball & basket-ball.

< CALLED BACK: (Left message) What is her name and phone number?

> TR: 1-[9**] xxx-####

< CALLED BACK: (Left message) What is her name?

> TR: E............ ....

< CALLED BACK: (Left message) Thanks!

> TR: I also gave K the information.

DELETED (I called E........ .... and left message.)

It has been about two months now so I will stop here temporarily and take stock of how things are progressing so far.

SUBTOTALS
JUNE 25–AUGUST 31 2015

94	INCOMING TEXT MESSAGES
7	MESSAGE NOT FOR ME [7%]
22	CALLED BACK [23%]
32	DELETED RIGHT AWAY [34%]
4	FOWARDED MESSAGE [4%]
12	*SAVED [12%]
21	TEXTED BACK [22%]
5	I SENT A PICTURE
0	I SENT INITIAL TEXTED MESSAGE

*10 were pictures of grandson

So far haven't proven much one way or the other. I am immediately deleting a little over one-third of incoming text messages. I have responded to about 50% of them by either calling back [23%], forwarding [4%], or texting back [22%] of the time. 7% of the text messages were not even intended for me.

I have not sent a text over three words long. My most popular text answers are "Yes/Yep" and "OK." I am also proud to say I have not sent an initial text message, unless you count pictures, but I never attach a message to those.

BACK TO THE TEXT LOG

September 2, 2015
> JG: Hey coach! Tell the   DELETED (I told the girls.)
girls I said good luck tonight
and I miss them.
> JJ: How'd it go?   < CALLED BACK (We talk-
                                          ed about our games.)

September 3, 2015
> E: Thank you!   < CALLED BACK (I didn't
                                          know what this was about.)
> KL: A, M, E & I are watch-   DELETED
ing college football. Just
letting you know.

September 9, 2015
> KL: Remember it is S's   DELETED
birthday tomorrow she
wants chocolate cupcakes.

September 11, 2015
                                          < TEXTED KB: Volleyball
                                          scores from Rochester Tour-
                                          nament, 2 matches.
> KB: Yay!   < CALLED BACK: (Left mes-
                                          sage) "Give me a break; that
                                          took me 10 minutes!"

September 12, 2015
                                          < TEXTED KB: Volleyball
> KB: Captain obvious, thank   scores from Rochester Tour-
you for the voice message.   nament. Left voicemail also.
To save you all the duress
next time please let K do it
next time. Drive safe!
> LB: Sent picture of grand-   SAVED
son.
> KB: Thanks!   DELETED

> KB: No thank you!   DELETED (I don't know
                                       who this is for.)

September 14, 2015
> KB: If you use the music   < CALLED BACK: (Left mes-
today, can you wheel it into   sage) I'm not using it.
my office when done? I need
it for class tonight.
> JL: Good luck tonight!   DELETED (We are not play-
                                      ing tonight.)

> LB: Sent pictures of grand-   SAVED
son.

September 16, 2015
> JJ: Call me.   < CALLED BACK
> LB: Sent picture of grand-   SAVED
son

September 23, 2015
> KW: we are getting ad-   < CALLED BACK (Left ad-
dresses for our Save the   dress on message.)
Date, what is yours?
> LB: Sent picture of grand-   < SAVED/TEXTED: Please
son.   send to my computer.

September 25, 2015

                                     < TEXTED KB: Volleyball
                                     scores from the NDSCS
                                     Tournament Day #1.
> KB: Have a goodnight!   DELETED
> KW: Thanks!   DELETED
                                     < Sent GM pictures from
                                     NDSCS Tournament.
September 26, 2015

                                     < TEXTED KB: Scores from
                                     NDSCS Tournament Day #2.

September 29, 2015
> JJ: I'll call you in a few.   Never did call (I called back.)

September 30, 2015
> JL: Our van is in the shop,   DELETED
so we walked to our dental
appointment. I don't know if
we can walk to the college. I
want bikes.

> JJ: We lost in 5.   DELETED (I had called ask-
ing before.)

October 1, 2015
> EG: Hi coach, sorry I   < CALLED BACK
missed your call the other
day, did you need some-
thing?

October 5, 2015
> LR: Call mom when you   < CALLED my mom.
get a chance, she has had
some tough days… a lot of
back and leg pain.

    < CALLED recruit and left
    message.

> R: Sorry I missed your call,   < CALLED BACK: (Left mes-
I'm on a volleyball bus right   sage) I hope you won!
now.

> R: Yes we won.   < TEXTED R: Is there a good
    time to call you?

> R: Tomorrow night.   < TEXTED BACK: ok
    < CALLED BACK NEXT
    DAY (We talked.)

October 6, 2015
> ED: So sorry not to have
been able to receive your
last few phone calls. I have
been having trouble with my
phone not receiving calls or
not being notified of missed
calls until many hours later. I

13

am getting it fixed tomorrow however.

October 8, 2015
> TR: Do you know of a camera we can use this weekend for our scrimmage?
> TR: 10:15 AM Who is the Librarian?

< TEXTED TR: Check with the library.

DELETED (10:00 PM *I haven't looked at my phone all day.)

October 10, 2015
> RP: You won $25 from Zaverls'!
> RP: We already used it.

< TEXTED RP: Big night!

< TEXTED BACK: OK, as long as it wasn't M!

> RP: He won the other $25!
< TEXTED BACK: Use his!

October 12, 2015
> TR: How do I log into Hurdle?

< CALLED BACK: (Left message) It is HUDL, I'll check. (Emailed info later.)

> TR: Hudl?
DELETED

October 17, 2015

< Sent MF pictures of Kansas & Texas Tech football game.
October 18, 2015

> KB: If you are coming in today let me know, work keys in the laundry room.
DELETED (I'm in Nebraska, she'll remember.)

> KB: Practicing?
< CALLED BACK: (Left message) I'm in Nebraska.

> KB: Never mind.
DELETED

One phone call could have covered this.

October 19, 2015
> CC: Hey coach, I just got
< CALLED BACK: (Left mes-

14

home, I have a cyst on my ovary.

sage) Call me.

> CC: Hey coach, I'm going to stay home today.

< TEXTED BACK: Get well!

> CC: Thank you coach.

DELETED

Again, one phone call!

October 20, 2015

> R: Thank you for considering me for Hibbing

< CALLED BACK (Wished her all the best!)

October 21, 2015

< Sent B pictures to send to my computer.

October 23, 2015

> PM: Hi, I just went back into my junk mail. Not sure why your email came in as junk. I will start on the plaques right now.

< CALLED BACK

October 29, 2015

> JJ: Thanks for the good luck email. I emailed you back from my phone but the emails are not sending.

DELETED

October 30, 2015

> KL: Central Lakes won in 3 and Mesabi won in 4.

DELETED

I don't email from my phone, only on my computer at work.

That is another two months of flip phone activity so let's run some numbers.

SUB TOTALS SEPTEMBER 2 – OCTOBER 30 2015

45	INCOMING TEXT MESSAGES
1	MESSAGE NOT FOR ME [2%]
14	CALLED BACK [31%]
17	DELETED RIGHT AWAY [37%]
0	FORWARDED MESSAGE [0%]
4	*SAVED [8%]
7	TEXTED BACK [15%]
3	I SENT A PICTURE
4	**I SENT INITIAL TEXT MESSAGE

* All pictures of my grandson.
** All volleyball scores I had to report.

In comparing the first two months with the third and fourth months, here are a few observations: I increased my immediate DELETE rate from 34% to 37%. Points for me! I dropped my TEXTING BACK rate from 22% to 15%. Another pat on the back for me. I CALLED BACK 31% of the time compared to 23% earlier. I'll attribute that to less time at the lake. I responded with a TEXT, CALL BACK, or FORWARD 46% of the time, down from 50% the first two months. A lot more trivial messages this time around.

On my end: I sent one less picture and only SAVED four messages, again all pictures of my grandson. My daughter needs to step it up.

Most noticeably I initialized four text messages. Don't judge me; I had to. They were all volleyball scores I had to report.

New record: the longest text message I sent was eight words long.

FIRST FOUR
MONTH TOTALS

JUNE 25 – OCTOBER 30, 2015

139	INCOMING TEXT MESSAGES
8	MESSAGES NOT FOR ME [5%]
36	CALLED BACK [25%]
49	DELETED RIGHT AWAY [35%]
4	FORWARDED MESSAGE [2%]
16	*SAVED [11%]
28	TEXTED BACK [20%]
8	I SENT A PICTURE
4	**I SENT INITIAL TEXT MESSAGE

* 14 were pictures of my grandson.

** All volleyball scores I had to report.

BACK TO THE TEXT LOG

November 1, 2015
> LB: Sent pictures of grand-   SAVED
son.

November 2, 2015
> LR: Don't forget it is   DELETED (Called my mom.)
mom's 81st birthday today.

November 4, 2015
> KB: AS is not playing bas-   DELETED (Knew that, not
ketball next year.   this year either.)

> JJ: Scan of an email, phone   DELETED (Saw her half
number for conference call   hour ago and asked her to do
tomorrow morning.   this.)
                                   < CALLED JJ: (left message)
                                   Call me with a number;
                                   I can't read it on my flip
                                   phone.
> BS: Sent phone number for   SAVED
conference call
> JJ: BS just sent it.   < TEXTED BACK: Got it,
                                   thanks!

> JJ: You are the only one he   DELETED
forgot in the north.   < TEXTED BS: Thanks!
> JJ: You were not on the to: DELETED
list
> BS: No Mike, thank you!   < TEXTED BACK: You're an
                                   ass!
> BS: Well, just saying   < TEXTED BACK: 9:57 PM
                                   Go to bed!

November 6, 2015
> BS: 7:36 AM Waky Waky,   < TEXTED BACK: You are
Eggs and Baky!   such a mom! Microphone
                                   down!

> JJ: D, C & B didn't get emails for conference call

DELETED (Called conference commissioner last night to make sure he has my email right.)

November 8, 2015

< CALLED GP and left message to call me.

> GP: Who is this?

< TEXTED BACK: Mike Turnbull; call me.

> GP (Called me back & we talked)

Imagine that, we talked and it only took two texted messages to get to a phone conversation!

November 10, 2015
> KB: With no school tomorrow our team is hoping to practice from 11:00-1:00. I'm checking with T, but don't know if he is back. I'm assuming it will be okay, but if you know different, please let me know.

DELETED (Walked over to her office and talked to her.)

November 12, 2015

< TEXTED LS: Tough one today! Good luck tomorrow. Coach Turnbull HCC Volleyball
< TEXTED JD: Hang in there! Good luck tomorrow. Coach Turnbull HCC Volleyball

> JD: Thanks! Will do.

DELETED
< TEXTED AS: Now you guys can just relax & play. Good luck tomorrow! Coach

	Turnbull HCC Volleyball
> AS: We sure will! Thank you!	DELETED

November 13, 2015

	< TEXTED AS: Great season! Coach Turnbull HCC Volleyball < TEXTED JD: Be proud! Best season in your school's history! Coach Turnbull HCC Volleyball < TEXTED LS: Be proud! No matter how many Cook County teams go to state, you can always say you played for the first. Coach Turnbull HCC Volleyball
> JD: Thank you! It was a great experience!	DELETED
> AS: Thank you! It was fun!	DELETED

November 14, 2015

> LS: Thank you!	< CALLED BACK (Left message.)
> MF: WEM won in 5. 15-13	DELETED (Knew that!)

November 16, 2015

> Unknown: Do you need a transfer form for a player if they were not full time?	DELETED (I don't think this was for me.)
> P: I do not believe so.	DELETED (Not for me.)
> Unknown: Thanks	DELETED (Can't fool me.)

Again, why am I in this group message?

November 17, 2015
> TR: How do I put stats on

the NJCAA site?

< CALLED BACK: (Left message) go to Presto Sports and enter the stats.

> BS: Nothing!

DELETED (I'm ignoring him.)

> BS: You are such a mom! Microphone down!

DELETED (Still ignoring him.)

> JJ: My cousin teaches in HCC Dental program will drop off TR's game film.

< CALLED BACK: (Left message) I won't be here.

Question: Why is it that if I call someone back right after they texted me I never get an answer and I have to leave a message?

> R: Hey coach, I'm sorry I haven't returned your calls. I don't have my phone on when you call. I'm doing homework. I'm leaning toward St. Scholastica or Mesabi for engineering. I'm keeping my options open. Can't seem to decide right now.

< CALLED BACK (Discussed plans for next year.)

November 20, 2015

< CALLED AT&T for a phone #

> AT&T: [218] 262-xxxx

November 22, 2015
> MR: Did I forget anything? Look at the free turkey, courtesy Cargill. Go Vikes! Attached picture of groceries.

DELETED (Why did I get this?)

> LR: Wow!

DELETED (Again, why did I get this?)

> Unknown: Thanks for hosting.

DELETED (I have no idea)

> Unknown: Thanks for all your hard work see you Thursday!

DELETED (Thanksgiving?)

November 28, 2015
> TR: Are you around 4:20ish?

<TEXTED TR: I could be?
<TEXTED R: Have you sent back your LOI?

November 29, 2015
> JL: just remembered you were supposed to call soon. Could you call tomorrow night around same time. I came home from work sick, took some Nyquil and I am going to bed

< TEXTED BACK: I will. Get well! (Called next night.)

December 1, 2015
> TR: Where did you get those jackets last year?

< CALLED BACK (Left message) Custom Lettering.
< TEXTED R: have you sent back your LOI yet?

> R: I never got it

< TEXTED BACK: I sent it 11/19 in the mail. Check your email for a second copy. Please sign it and send it back ASAP.

> R: ok

< TEXTED BACK: Thanks

December 2, 2015

< Sent LB picture of my new truck.

> LB: Congrats! Is it blue?
> LB: Nice!
> B: Sent picture of a bottle of New York Seltzer Pop bottle.

< TEXTED BACK: lazer blue!
DELETED
< CALLED BACK (Talked. Great conversation about how this was his favorite when he was little. Had found some in a store in Minneapolis.)

December 3, 2015

> R: I faxed it to you just now.	< TEXTED BACK: Got it, thanks! (I had called her about LOI.)
> R: Yep!	DELETED (Called back.)

December 6, 2015

> LB: Sent picture of grandson.	SAVED
> Unknown: Message about Apple ID#	DELETED (I do nothing with Apple.)
> B: Must be like you getting stuck in the snow to mark the tree.	DELETED (This was for his sister.)
> LB: Ha, Ha, except no snow & we didn't abandon him.	DELETED (This is my son & daughter going back and forth.)
> LB: Well they were kind of short, thanks though.	DELETED (This was to my wife.)

Again, another group message; okay to be a part of it this time!

December 8, 2015

> TR: I want a copy of both your books. Can I buy them through you or should I go through Amazon?	< TEXTED BACK: I have both. Deal $20. I'll leave them on your desk.
> TR: Ok I am on my way there.	DELETED
> TR: What's up?	DELETED (Not for me.)
> TR: Nothing, wrong person.	DELETED
> TR: Want me to put the $20 on your desk?	< TEXTED BACK: Sure! Thanks!
> TR: You coming back tonite?	< TEXTED BACK: About 8:00
> TR: No rush, looking forward to the read!	DELETED (Dropped off books, no money on my desk.)

This could have all been done with one phone call!

> KB: Good news! MG just joined our HCC Athletic page, after saying she was going to Mesabi.

DELETED (What the hell?)

December 11, 2015
> R: Hey this is J, I've been busy every time you have called. I haven't decided yet where I am going.

CALLED BACK (Left message)

> JL: Hi coach, I'm running for Winter Frolic this year & I'm selling buttons, they are $3. Wondering if you would like to buy any?

< TEXTED BACK: I'll take 2.

< Sent B, LB, P pictures of fire-place project at cabin.

December 12, 2015

< Sent B, LB, P, & MF pictures of deer in front yard of cabin.

> MF: I should deer hunt out your cabin window.

DELETED

> LB: Nice! What is the pic with the ceiling fan?

< CALLED BACK (Talked for ½ hour.)

< Sent MF more deer pictures. They won't leave the birdfeeders alone.

> MF: Nice!

December 13, 2015
> LB: Sent pictures of grandson sitting with Santa

SAVED: (TEXTED: Please send to my computer!)

> A: Cute! I like his shoes.

DELETED (Not for me.)

> LB: Yep! He is a big boy now!

DELETED (Not for me.)

December 14, 2015

< Sent L, M, S, T, and JJ Christ-

mas pictures of my grandson.

December 15, 2015
> LR: Thanks! This made my day! Beautiful picture!

DELETED

> JJ: Awesome, Adorable! Thanks for sharing!

DELETED

> MR: Hey Mike, you called last night & I missed it. What's up?

DELETED (I was just trying to bug him during the Adele TV special.)

> B: 6401 France Ave. S/ N's number is XXXXXXX

(I had called him because I was going to Minneapolis to see my best friend in hospital, needed address.)

> LB: Video of grandson decorating Christmas tree.

SAVED

December 16, 2015
> MR: Did you call me to just let my phone ring? No message. No texted reply. Too old to remember why you called in the first place?

< CALLED BACK (Told him I was just messing with him during Adele show.)

< Sent my mom pictures of my grandson.

< Sent D picture of grandson.

December 18, 2015

< CALLED KL to see why she wasn't at game to work. Left message.

> KL: Got your message and totally forgot but I'll make it for sure tomorrow. Sorry!!

< TEXTED BACK: Thanks! Remind M also, 12:30 on Saturday.

> KL: Will do.

DELETED

December 19, 2015
> MM: That is probably the cutest Santa picture I've ever seen!

DELETED (I sent her the picture of Santa and my grandson

last week.)

December 21, 2015

< Sent P, L, and B pictures of Christmas lights outside of cabin

> LB: It is magical!   DELETED (She'll be here December 23rd.)

> PT: So   < CALLED BACK (She had no idea what that was about.)

Side note: Been meaning to write this down. Did anyone else notice that at the beginning of the Adele Live in New York show on NBC that she took a phone call in a limousine and she had a flip phone? Proud moment for this flip phone owner.

December 24, 2015

> JG: Do you still have my stuff?   < CALLED BACK: (Left message) I have your stuff. I'll be back in Hibbing on

December 25, 2015   Saturday.

> TT: Merry Christmas to all!   < CALLED BACK: (Left message) Merry Christmas! Love you!

December 26, 2015

> DP: God is good! When I got to M's room he started to cry when I said I was there and how much I love him. He cried when he heard his mom. He is in there; he is in there!   DELETED (Said a prayer for M. Very dear friend in a coma. Left him a message on his phone; I hope someone plays it to him.)

December 27, 2015

> LB: Sent picture of grandson.   SAVED

> AK: Ahhh cute. Miss this little guy already.   DELETED (For LB.)

> LB: J said he is on his way via UPS.   DELETED (For LB.)

**That is two more months of activity on my cell phone.
Here are the numbers.**

NOVEMBER 1 – DECEMBER 27, 2015

83   INCOMING TEXT MESSAGES
9   MESSAGES NOT FOR ME [10%]
16 CALLED BACK [19%]
40 DELETED RIGHT AWAY [48%]
0   FORWARDED MESSAGE [0%]
6   *SAVED [7%]
18 TEXTED BACK [21%]
7   I SENT A PICTURE
7   **I SENT ORIGINAL TEXT MESSAGE

* 5 pictures of grandson & one phone number.

** All to recruits.

Comparing September and October to
November and December:

INCOMING TEXT MESSAGES: Up 38 (Please just call me.)
MESSAGES NOT FOR ME: Up 8% (Should I be developing a complex?)
CALLED BACK: Down 12% (I'm learning not to bother.)
DELETED RIGHT AWAY: Up 11% (Good for me!)
FORWARDED MESSAGE: (Still zero.)
SAVED: Down 1% (Still all but one was a picture of grandson; the other was a phone number.)
TEXTED BACK: Up 6% (What was I thinking?)
I SENT A PICTURE: Up 4 (Cabin and proud grandpa.)
I SENT INITIAL TEXT MESSAGE: Up 3 (Seven total, all to volleyball recruits.)

BACK TO THE TEXT LOG

JANUARY 1, 2016

> LB: Picture of grandson

SAVED (Great start to a new year!)

JANUARY 5, 2016

> JG: Can I get my stuff today?

< CALLED BACK: (Left message) I'll be back in Hibbing January 7th.

JANUARY 7, 2016

> TR: Phone number for coach in Michigan

DELETED (Wrote it down.)

> TT: I have a 2:00 appointment to look at Cedar's assisted living for mom.

DELETED

> LR: Great, I'll call this weekend.

DELETED (Not for me!)

< TEXTED LP: L, have you decided on a school for next year? And/or are you still interested in Hibbing CC? Coach Turnbull
< TEXTED JG: Call me. (She never did. I still have her stuff.)

JANUARY 8, 2016

> PS: Mike, heading to Nebraska next week. Thanks again for setting us up.

< CALLED BACK (Talked for a while. He is hunting on my son-in-law's family farm.)

> TT: What a lovely place and reasonable. We need to help mom make a decision. Let's talk tomorrow.

DELETED (I'll call tomorrow.)

> LR: Thanks T. We are going to check assisted Living in Maple Grove.

DELETED (Not for me, but I'll call her too.)

> TT: Still, call me.

DELETED (Not for me.)

> TT: Two rooms open at $1,125 per month plus meals.

DELETED (I'll call her tomorrow.)

> LP: I have been accepted to UW-Stout and Eau Claire. So I'm deciding between those two. Thanks for recruiting me. Good luck next year.
> TT: I am off tomorrow.
> KB: Let me know if K played tonight.
> LR: Okay, I'll call tomorrow.
> LP: Thank you very much!

< TEXTED BACK: Thanks! If anything changes contact me. Good luck to you.

DELETED
CALLED BACK (K had not played.)
DELETED (Not for me.)
DELETED (Have to move on to other recruits.)

January 9, 2016
> KB: Game was suspended. There is 5:45 left, shot clock stopped working. We were winning all game and were ahead 64-60. D refused to play without shot clock. Even though the men said they would play the next game without one. He is waiting to get K back again and then they will reschedule. I've never been more disappointed!

DELETED (I had called her and left message and asked how game went. She is pissed; I'll see her on Monday.)
< CALLED BACK (Left message to call me.)

January 11, 2016
> Unknown: Hey coach I'm thinking about going to Hibbing next year! When would it be best to tour?
> Unknown: This is TS

< TEXTED Unknown: Who is this? Coach Turnbull HCC Volleyball

< TEXTED BACK: Great I will call again later tonight.

Is it just me, or could this have all been covered with one phone call?

> LB: Picture of my grandson
> AK: Yay!

SAVED
DELETED (Not for me.)
< TEXTED CW: Roll Tide!

> CW: OMG! A text from Coach T

> MJ: Coach sorry I have been playing every time you have called.

(Sent after Alabama scored first touchdown against Clemson.) DELETED

CALLED BACK (For the 5th time in 3 days. No voicemail box set up.)

January 12, 2016
> TR: Softball meeting at 4:00 in PE-104 today see any girls you can think of let them know to come.

DELETED (Emailed my volley-ball players and let them know.)

January 13, 2015
> PT: Sent picture of Lynx in front yard at cabin.

SAVED

January 16, 2016
> JL: Just a reminder, T is at Mayo again this week we will leave tomorrow. Plan to be back late Wednesday night and be in clinic Thursday and Friday and games on weekend.

< CALLED BACK to make sure everything was okay with T.

> Unknown: Thanks good luck with everything.

DELETED (Not for me.)

> GP: Mike any word on prop-erty next door?

< CALLED BACK (Talked about it. Somebody is buying it.)

> TT: Got your message. Look-ing forward to seeing you on Thursday night. Thanks for bringing chairs. Still thinking about chair from Mom. I'll call before Wednesday.

< CALLED BACK: I'm leaving Wednesday.

January 18, 2016
> TT: I am going to get the   DELETED
couch, rocker and your recliner.
> JL: G's number is [218] xxx-   SAVED to contacts.
xxxx

January 22, 2016
> JS: Give me a call   CALLED BACK (Discussed
                                      2016 Volleyball schedule.)

January 25, 2016
> LB: Sent 7-month picture of   SAVED & TEXTED BACK:
my grandson.   Please send to my computer.
> LB: Already did!   DELETED

January 26, 2016
> MF: Just an FYI. I'm staying   DELETED (Got message at end
home today. I have a very sick   of day.)
daughter at home. She is having
migraines and throwing up.
Fun...Fun.

January 27, 2016
> JS: Scan of an email I can't   DELETED & TEXTED BACK:
read on my flip phone.   What is this?
> JS: We can play 22 dates next   DELETED (I found this out
year.   three days ago.)

February 1, 2016
> AT&T: Phone number for   SAVED (Needed to remind C I
college switchboard   was in Nebraska.)

February 2, 2016
> R: Hey! I'm doing a phone-   DELETED (I had left a message
a-thon for dollars for scholars   for her. She never did call back.)
right now, so I can't talk on the
phone, I'll get back to you.

February 5, 2016

> KB: I'll call you back in a bit.

DELETED (I had called to see if she had heard anything from A.)

> KB: AG [715] XXX-XXXX

< TEXTED BACK: Thanks! (I had asked her to text me AG's number.)
< TEXTED A: A, please call me when you get a chance. Coach Turnbull (I had already called several times.)
< TEXTED B and AK: Picture of grandson.
< TEXTED picture of grandson to my computer.

February 7, 2016

> PT: Picture of grandson.

SAVED
< TEXTED PT: Picture of grandson.
< TEXTED three pictures of grandson to my computer.

February 9, 2016

> KB: I'm going to the Floodwood NK game tonight. So if you want me to bring M's LOI, I could have her sign it tonight.

DELETED (Talked to KB at school, gave her the LOI.)
< TEXTED MJ: M, Coach B is bringing your LOI to your game tonight. She will have you sign it after your game. Good Luck tonight! Coach Turnbull (I hope she reads this because I'll never get the five minutes back that it took to send this text.)

> MJ: Thanks! (I didn't need those 5 minutes.)

DELETED

< TEXTED TC: I will be in Ely this Thursday through Tuesday nights, if there are any games you want me to help with.

> TC: Mike, VCC game 3:00 Saturday & Hockey

< TEXTED BACK: Sounds good, what time is the hockey game Friday night?

> TC: 7:30

< TEXTED BACK: OK I'll be there for both. (I should have just called and taken care of all this in one conversation.)

> KB: Got your LOI signed… she's gonna fill out the size sheet later. EH was there we all talked for a long time. I think she'll play basketball too. We have to get MA to come to our campus.

DELETED (Called KB.)

> TC: Perfect

DELETED

February 10, 2016

> LB: Picture of grandson

SAVED (Sent to my computer.)

> BT: Ha Ha looks like a different occupation would make him happier.

DELETED (Not for me.)

> AT: Cute!!

DELETED (Not for me.)

> PT: He doesn't look that happy about it. Next time it will have to be an up north outfit.

DELETED (Not for me.)

> PT: Put his hat on next time to complete the ensemble. Every farmer needs a hat.

DELETED (Not for me.)

> AT: or a tuxedo.

DELETED: (Not for me.)

> LB: I know he was not happy in his car seat today.

DELETED: (Not for me.) (I really do hate it when I get caught in a group text.)

February 11, 2016

> LB: Video of grandson crawling.

SAVED (Sent to my computer.)

> PT: Does he move?

DELETED (Not for me.)

> LB: Yes, I know it is hard to see. I sent it to your email also.

DELETED (Not for me.)

> LB: Video of grandson crawl-
ing.

SAVED

February 12, 2016
> LR: Do you guys want the
blonde dresser?

< TEXTED BACK: Call P.

February 14, 2016
> LB: Valentine's picture of
grandson.

SAVED

> PT: Best Valentine's ever!
Yours should be in mail in a
couple of days. Love you guys!

DELETED (Not for me.)

> JL: We are in Ely today. Sug-
gestions on where to eat? My
nephew is playing hockey.

CALLED BACK (Too late, they
were already at the Steakhouse.)

February 15, 2016

< Sent PT, BT, and LB pictures
of kitchen cabinets at cabin.
< Sent picture of my grandson
to my computer.

> KL: K's number is [763] XXX-
XXXX.

< TEXTED BACK: Thanks! (I
had called her and asked for K's
number.)

February 16, 2016
> TR: Hey I have to send in
nominations for all-division. I
am not sure how this works can
you tell me how many I get? I
don't want to screw anybody
and I don't want to nominate
too many. Thoughts?

CALLED BACK: (Talked about
it.)

February 19, 2016
> TC: Game postponed, playing
tomorrow but no radio.

DELETED (Was supposed to
broadcast Ely -vs- Chisholm

game. Postponed due to weather.)

February 20, 2016
> KB: Not a good day, we lost by 20 and the men lost by 40.

< TEXTED BACK: Thanks. Drive safe! (I had called her to see how games went between HCC & CLC.)
< Sent pictures to my computer for my book.

February 21, 2016
> TC: Doing VCC game on Friday in Anoka. You are welcome to come if you want.
> TC: Thanks got the message. Tell P good luck.

DELETED (Called back, left message.)

DELETED

February 23, 2016
> LB: 8 Month picture of grandson: He was home sick today GJ watched him.
> PT: What sort of sick?

SAVED: Sent it to my computer

DELETED (Not for me. Called PT.)

> LB: Just a cold but he did have a slight fever yesterday so he had to stay home from daycare today.
> PT: He sure looks cute. Maybe it is his teeth.
> LB: Yeah, that's what we thought.

DELETED (Not for me.)

DELETED (Not for me.)

DELETED (Not for me. I guess it was ok to be in on these messages.)

February 24, 2016
> JJ: Hi coach, I got asked to play for JO Volleyball Minnesota North team. I am just texting to make sure that I am allowed to play.

< TEXTED BACK: Definitely yes!

February 24, 2016

< TEXTED CW: Good luck tonite! Coach

> CW: Thanks coach!

February 26, 2016

< TEXTED AT: A, just heard the good news. Congrats! Mike

> AT: Thanks Mike!!

February 29, 2016
> TC: Are you in Hibbing? I'm doing the girl's game at 5:45.

< TEXTED BACK: Sorry I missed this, I was at baseball practice. (8:00 PM)

> TC: No problem. Ely girls won in OT.

That is two more months of activity on my flip phone. Let's stop and check the numbers.

JANUARY 1, 2016- FEBRUARY 29, 2016

79   INCOMING TEXT MESSAGES

19   MESSAGES NOT FOR ME [24%]

12   CALLED BACK [15%]

43   DELETED RIGHT AWAY [54%]

0   FORWARDED MESSAGE [0%]

12   SAVED [15%]

12   TEXTED BACK [15%]

7   I SENT A PICTURE

11   I SENT ORIGINAL TEXT

COMPARING JAN-FEB to NOV-DEC
INCOMING TEXTS: Down 4
MESSAGES NOT FOR ME: Up 14% (Group messaging @#&$*)
CALLED BACK: Down 4%
DELETED RIGHT AWAY: Up 6% (Good for me!)
FORWARDED MESSAGE: 0 (Nothing worth sharing.)
SAVED: Up 8% (More pictures of grandson.)
TEXTED BACK: Down 6% (Again, good for me!)
I SENT A PICTURE: SAME
I SENT ORIGINAL TEXT: Up 4 (What am I doing?)

BACK TO THE LOG

March 1, 2016

> LB: Picture of grandson: One little quick B fix before you go on your trip. He got his hair styled yesterday.	SAVED
> PT: Little Mohawk & his poor little red nose. He is still adorable. I'll show E this one and see if he thinks there is any likeness.	DELETED (Not for me.)
> LB: The red nose was from eating sweet potatoes. But yes please show him.	DELETED (Not for me.)
> PT: He is looking like a pretty big boy in that high chair.	DELETED (Not for me.)
> LB: Agreed, he is way ahead of EW.	DELETED (Not for me.)
> PT: Way to go B. He is going to be all grown up next time we see him.	DELETED (Not for me.)
> LB: I know if he is not walking I'll be shocked!	DELETED (Not for me.)
> PT: Tie him down until June.	DELETED (Not for me.)
> LB: I'll do my best!	DELETED (NOT FOR ME!)
> PT: Talk to you soon! Love you guys!	DELETED (Still not for me!)
> LB: Us too. Have a great trip!	DELETED (I'll take that one.) My wife and daughter need to get their own group. All I needed was the picture!

March 2, 2016

	< Sent picture of my grandson to my computer.
> LR: Zeroez carpet cleaner is scheduled for the afternoon of March 8th. Check it off the list.	DELETED (From my sister; my mom's condo is getting cleaned.)

> SJ: Thanks for setting this up.   DELETED (Not for me.)

March 5, 2016
> PT: Picture of me and Nan   SAVED
Wooden at UCLA game.   < Sent KB & MF picture from
                                  PT.
> KB: What a special day, hope   DELETED
you're having a great time.   < Sent MR, KB, & MF another
                                  picture from UCLA game.
> MF: Nice to see you were able   < CALLED BACK: It was his
to talk to Coach W's sister! But I daughter!
like the other pic better.   < Sent BT pictures from UCLA
                                  game.
March 6, 2016
                                  < Sent BT picture of me by
                                  John Wooden statue on UCLA
                                  campus.
> LB: By the way B pulled   DELETED
himself up in his crib today.
Nice head shot on the monitor.
I don't think he'll need a wagon
for the wedding.
> AC: Yay!   < Sent AC pictures of succu-
                                  lents.
                                  DELETED (Not for me.)
> MR: Great seats! Who cares   DELETED
who is playing.
> LB: Video of grandson.   SAVED
> LR: Glad you are having a   < CALLED BACK
great time! Don't forget to get
chairs and blue tub before you
leave mom's. That will help with
storage.
                                  < TEXTED SJ: Yes, thanks. (She
                                  had called.)
> MR: How was the game last   < CALLED BACK
night? Was the pic of the cheer-

39

leader from your seats or did you run down there? How did you get in the Pauley Room?

> MF: Why do you keep sending me the same two pictures?	DELETED (I don't know.)
	< Sent MF picture of JW statue.
> MF: Ok there is a new one!	DELETED
> MJ: Awesome!	DELETED
> SJ: Sent picture of JW statue & me.	SAVED
> SJ: Sent picture of JW statue, her, and me.	SAVED
> SJ: More pictures from UCLA game.	SAVED
> SJ: Did you get the picture?	< TEXTED BACK: Yes, thanks!

Let me explain: My wife and I are in California on vacation. My sister arranged for us to go to a UCLA Men's Basketball game. Set it up with a booster. VIP treatment: Pauley Room, met Nan Wooden, and sat in baseline seats. An unbelievable experience. Way too special to really explain. I'll never be able to thank her enough!

March 7, 2016

	< Sent AC pictures of succulents. My wife said she likes them.
> AC: Succulents, very cool!	< Sent AC more pictures of succulents.
> AC: Awesome! [I guess she does like them.	DELETED
> AC: I hope you guys are having a great time.	< TEXTED BACK: Going well. P has been in Hearst Castle for 4 hours, I did the one hour tour.
> AC: Ha! Ha! Of course!	DELETED
	< Sent several people pictures of Elephant Seals on the beach. (I'm killing time while my wife

> MF: Holy crap those things are fat! By the way my wife was talking to DF. His daughter wants to play volleyball at HCC.
> SJ: Nice!
> SJ: Are they sleeping?

is touring Hearst Castle.)
< CALLED BACK

DELETED
< TEXTED BACK: No
< Sent several people pictures of Pacific Coast drive.
< Sent MR, BT, & MJ pictures of Pebble Beach.

> MR: No I have never been there. You are killing me!
> MJ: Looks like you are missing coaching baseball!
> MR: Some day! Enjoy the view. How did you Hit them?

DELETED

DELETED

DELETED (He knows I don't golf.)

March 8, 2016
> TR: I just got off the phone with two girls from Hawaii, they want to play volleyball.
> PT: Pictures from vacation.

< CALLED BACK: (Left message) We'll talk when I get back from California.
SAVED

March 10, 2016

< Sent my sisters pictures from our old neighborhood in Alameda, CA

> AC: Hope all is well. Just wanted to check what terminal and what time you are arriving. B said 12:30.
> PT: We are at Alcatraz. 12:30, I'll get back to you about what terminal. Having a great time.
> AC: Ok sounds good.

DELETED (Not for me.)

DELETED (Not for me.)

DELETED (Not for me.)

> LB: Picture of grandson's first shiner.	SAVED
> PT: Did he get it at daycare?	DELETED (Not for me.)
> LU: Dirt nap?	< TEXTED BACK: ?
> LR: Cool!	
	< Sent LR more pictures of Alameda.
> TT: What are the gray houses?	< Sent TT more Alameda pictures.
	< Sent KB pictures of Brewery in Alameda.

March 11, 2016

> PT: Picture of Navy Base gate.	SAVED
> AM: Hey Coach T, L wants to know if she can bring a friend to open gym.	< TEXTED BACK: Yes
> AM: One more question, can I change one of the songs on the volleyball CD?	< TEXTED BACK: Yes
> AM: OK	
	< TEXTED TT: It is where we lived.
> TT: I thought so.	DELETED
> TT: Is the Navy Base completely abandoned?	DELETED (Sent more pictures.)
	< Sent pictures of Turnbull Winery in Napa Valley to several people.
> LR: Did you go here?	DELETED (I am in the picture in front of the sign.)
> MF: Yesterday?	< TEXTED BACK: Yes

March 12, 2016

	< Accidentally sent MP picture of my grandson.
> TT: How great, looks like P & you are having a great time in	DELETED (I'll call her when we get home.)

California. More book material?   DELETED
> MF: Nice!
> KB: You found your next   DELETED
calling.
> BT: Just reffed AT's game. K   DELETED (Talked later.)
was coaching.

**We got back from our vacation on March 13th. Hopefully
all this texting insanity will stop for a while now.**

March 14, 2016
> MF: AF's number is [612]   SAVED number
XXX-XXXX

March 15, 2016
                                    < Sent two vacation pictures to
                                    my computer.
> TT: Mom said you intend to   DELETED (I will email her
visit her, but can't remember   tonight. I just told my mom two
what day you are coming. When   days ago.)
will you be visiting?

March 16, 2016
> TR: I slipped my bracket for   DELETED
the pool under your door.
> TT: I will be going to moms'   DELETED
this Friday til Saturday.
> LR: Sounds great! She says   DELETED (Not for me.)
you are taking grocery shop-
ping. Thanks! She also wants to
get her hair cut, appreciate your
help.

March 17, 2016
> TT: Happy to.   DELETED (Not for me.)
> TT: You guys have a safe and   DELETED (Not for me.)
wonderful trip!
> LR: Thanks, love you!   DELETED (Not for me.)

> TT: I love you too!

DELETED (Not for me.)
Another group message not for me. Unless my sisters are trying to make me feel guilty!
< Sent PT, LB, and BT pictures from cabin.

March 18, 2016

< Sent TT, LR, and SJ pictures from cabin.

> TT: Beautiful!

DELETED (Sent TT a picture of snow in Hibbing.)

> TT: Looks wet & heavy.

< TEXTED BACK: Yep!

> LR: Wow!

DELETED

> SJ: Winter Wonderland?

DELETED (She lives in Los Angeles, CA.)

March 20, 2016
> MF: Today

DELETED (Have no idea what this is!)

> MF: Hey coach, K can't open up in the morning Because L has a doctor's appointment. Can you be in by 8:00 to open the bike room, weight room and small gym?
> MF: Thanks!

< TEXTED BACK: I'll be there.

March 23, 2016
> TT: Mom's code to get in the front door of the building is *_ _ _ _ . A realtor is showing mom's home between 4 & 5:00 tomorrow. You might have to knock really hard on mom's door tonight because she is exceptionally tired tonight due to having her taxes done today. Mom is looking forward to your visit.

DELETED (I actually know this already.)

> LB: Sent 9-month picture of grandson.

SAVED & SENT to my computer.

> AC: Awwww!

DELETED (Not for me.)

> TT: Are you at mom's?

< CALLED BACK (I had forgotten to call when I got there.)

March 27, 2016

> LB: Sent Easter picture of grandson.

SAVED & SENT to my computer.

> LB: Sent another Easter picture of grandson.

SAVED & SENT to my computer.

> PT: We have the cutest grandson! Can't wait to see you all Thursday.

DELETED (Not for me.)

> LB: Us either and yes you do have the cutest grandson!

March 30, 2016

> SJ: Hi everyone, mom's place has not sold yet. The people that looked at it on Monday are interested and may come back for a second showing. Hopefully they will make an offer. I just spoke with her agent.

DELETED (I had already called her.)

> LR: Great!

DELETED (Not for me.)

> LR: I'm not sure why you didn't put the items from the dresser back in the guest bedroom closet. Mom's back is in rough shape and I can't get there until after school and she might have a showing.

DELETED (I had already left her a message explaining why I didn't.)

April 1, 2016

> TR: When do you have open gyms? I was hoping to start having BB open gyms on Tuesday

< TEXTED BACK: April 5 & 6 at 8.

45

> TR: And you're done?

> TR: I was going to set up my schedule

and Thursday nights.
< CALLED BACK (Left a message.)
DELETED (Called back and talked. [Finally!])

April 3, 2016

< Sent PT, LB, & my computer pictures of grandson at Omaha Zoo.
< Sent DB picture of second base monument from the old Rosenblatt Stadium which is now in the expanded parking lot at the Omaha Zoo. It is a sad site for die hard CWS fans!

April 5, 2016
> TR: Okay I was going to start going open gyms Tuesday & Thursday. Rest of April.
> AM Hey coach, do you think we should cancel open gym? The roads are getting pretty bad already and not many people are coming now.

DELETED

< CALLED BACK (We cancelled, she texted everyone & I emailed them.)

April 12, 2016
> DH: Good Morning Mike: I hope you are all doing well! Just an update for you! Our field will not be ready until Friday! I walked it over to my A.D., who is also named Mike, and read it to him. Then checked with Grand Rapids Sports Complex and they believe they could be ready tomorrow but will call me

DELETED it.

to confirm! We could play at 3:00 PM as scheduled or if you are okay with it bump up to 2 & 4:00 to capture the most heat and get back a little earlier. They charge $75 a game and if you are okay with it we could split it. This will resolve all issues. T's schedule, a playable field, and location convenient for all. I'll call back in a few hours to confirm. Have a good day!

> DH: Sorry Mike, wrong Mike, too many Mikes in one athletic department. At least we know who the good looking one is!

DELETED (It would be too easy to pick on him.)

April 14, 2016

< Sent picture of timber wolf in front of our cabin to PT, LB, BT, and MF.

> BT: Throw some meat out there for him.

DELETED (That's just stupid!)

> MF: Should have shot his ass!

DELETED (I don't own a gun.)

< TEXTED MF TC's phone number.

> MF: Thanks!

DELETED

> MF: Saturday game at VCC 12:00 at H.S. field.

DELETED (I'll probably go.)

April 15, 2016

> AC: Happy Birthday Mike!

< TEXTED BACK: Thanks!

> MF: Happy Birthday! Game Sunday noon at Nyberg Field.

< TEXTED BACK: Thanks!

> SJ: Happy Birthday from the J's!

< TEXTED BACK: Thanks!

Fortunately, everyone else called me for my birthday, otherwise way too much texting back today.

April 16, 2016
> TR: Hey, P is in right field. Talk to her to keep her going.

DELETED: I was sitting outside the fence. I did what I could to help her.

April 17, 2016

< Sent pictures of timber wolf at cabin to my computer.

April 18, 2016
> CO: Thanks for the keys, I just picked them up.

< TEXTED BACK: You're welcome. Let me know if there is anything else you need.
DELETED

> CO: All is well. My son and I will probably move to the 3rd floor tomorrow. Thanks!

April 19, 2016
> CO: Checking in. My son is here and we will stay on the 3rd floor tomorrow. I wanted you to know the scoop.

< TEXTED BACK: Thanks! (My favorite text other than OK.)

April 20, 2016
> AT&T: [218] XXX-XXXX (Number for Sammy's Pizza)

SAVED number to my phone (I had called Directory Assistance at 411. For those of you who don't know that is how you do it without Google.)

April 22, 2016

< Sent PT, BT, and LB pictures of kitchen cabinets at the cabin.
DELETED

> BT: Looks great!

< TEXTED LB: Send me a picture of B. I need a fix. (B is my grandson.)

April 23, 2016
> LB: Picture of grandson: Here you go 10 months old today!

< TEXTED BACK: Thanks!

> DP: Meet at Sir G's?????   < TEXTED BACK: OK (My
    favorite text!)

> DP: 2 Empty squares   DELETED (I have no idea what
    this is supposed to be.)

Saw DP & MP at Sir G's and asked her what two empty squares mean on a texted message meant. She figured it out. Apparently my phone can't receive emojis. I knew I couldn't send them, but this is great news! More stress eliminated from my life. Not only do I not have to worry about what emoji to use, I don't have to figure out what incoming emojis represent. Matter of fact I had to ask Ashley, Michele and Sam how to spell emoji when I wrote this.

April 24, 2016

    < Sent picture of my grandson
    to my computer.

> MP: Nice if I could drink!   DELETED (Not for me.)

April 25, 2016
> LB: Sent pictures of grandson   SAVED
playing with a friend.
> BT: Looks like they enjoy leg   DELETED (Not for me.)
wrestling!
> LB: Haha, I know right?   DELETED (Not for me.)

April 26, 2016
> BT: Sent three scans of some-   DELETED (Called him.)
thing I can't read on my phone.

April 27, 2016
> BT: Picture from suite at   < TEXTED BACK: Nice! For
Twins' game.   work?
> BT: No, D's work.   < TEXTED BACK: D gets all the
    perks!
    < Sent picture from BT to my
    computer.

April 28, 2016

> LB: Sent video of grandson.	SAVED (Sent to my computer.)
> AC: Hahahahaha! OMG cute!	DELETED (Not for me.)
> LB: Sent another video of grandson trying to walk.	SAVED (Sent to my computer.)
> TT: Our guest room in the building has 2 double beds….. so if you and P ever want to stop on your travels to Nebraska you can stay there for $25. Also full bathroom and a TV.	< TEXTED BACK: Sounds great!

My wife provided another reason for keeping my flip phone tonight. She dropped her iPhone in the toilet; it fell out of her back pocket. Use your imagination—you'll figure it out. Anyway, it isn't working and will probably be expensive to replace.

My flip phone is usually in my front pocket when I have it on me, and I'm not worried about a toilet accident other than peeing on my leg. If it ever does happen, a replacement should be $40–$50 or maybe they'll just give it to me for free if they have any left.

April 29, 2016

> TR: You around?	CALLED BACK

April 30, 2016

> JL: So we had the guy from Fergus that coached from our dugout now this guy goes to the bullpen. Requesting a lined coaching box!	TALKED TO HER PERSONALLY (I was at the same game.) DELETED

* That is two more months, time to take inventory.

MARCH 1 2016–APRIL 30 2016

__126__ INCOMING TEXTS

__25__ MESSAGES NOT FOR ME [19%]

__13__ CALLED BACK [10%]

__69__ DELETED RIGHT AWAY [54%]

__0__ FORWARDED MESSAGE [0%]

__14__ *SAVED [11%]

__17__ TEXTED BACK [13%]

__25__ **I SENT A PICTURE

__1__ ***I SENT ORIGINAL TEXT

* Twelve were pictures of grandson.
** What can I say? We went on vacation.
*** Maybe I can get that down to zero in May and June.

COMPARING MAR-APR to JAN-FEB
INCOMING TEXTS: Up 47 (We were on vacation.)
MESSAGES NOT FOR ME: Down 5% (It is getting better.)
CALLED BACK: Down 5% (We were on vacation.)
DELETED RIGHT AWAY: Same
FORWARDED MESSAGE: Same
SAVED: Down 4% (Fewer pictures of grandson, picked up late.)
TEXTED BACK: Down 8% (Good for me.)
I SENT A PICTURE: Up 7 (We were on vacation.)
I SENT ORIGINAL TEXT: Down 10 (I sent one in the last two months; ultimate goal is "0"!)

BACK TO LOG:
Two more months to go!

May 1, 2016
> LB: Video of grandson walk-ing.   SAVED (Sent to my computer.)

> PT: L, M, B and I just watched   DELETED (Not for me.)
the video. No stopping him
now!
> LB: I know!   DELETED (Not for me.)
> 256447: G-XXXXXX is your   DELETED (I finally remem-
Google verification code.   bered to delete my Gmail
                                      account. I never use it.)

May 2, 2016
> MR: I'm on the bus and will   DELETED (I had called and left
call you back in 5 minutes.   message.)
> TT: I reserved the guest room   < TEXTED BACK: Thanks, do
for Saturday night.   we need to bring linens? (I had
                                      left her a voice message.)

May 3, 2016
> TT: No. All is there. I am hop-   DELETED
ing you can make it closer to 8
than 9:00. We know A will bark
with all the moving excitement.
Looking forward to seeing you
and B. I so appreciate you coming and hauling mom's stuff.
> PT: Hey, I'm filling out the size   < TEXTED BACK: Great!
sheet right now. Sending it soon,
thank you.
> PT: Can you let me know if   < TEXTED BACK: Got it.
you got it please. I just sent it.   Thanks! (Had to check my email
                                      first and emailed her back also.)

> MR: Your mom likes the idea   < TEXTED BACK: Right and it
of the couch but wants to see the   is comfortable.
picture first. I will stop by and
show her tonite and let you

know. She wants to make sure
it is firm and the bed is really
good for her guests. Queen size
bed... right?

May 4, 2016

> MR: Your mom says she
would love to get the couch. I
told her that meant lots of extra
work for you and she said she
didn't care! OK – maybe she
didn't throw that last part in.
I told her you are planning on
coming down to her place Friday night.

DELETED

> MR: Did you get my texted
about your mom wanting the
couch?

< TEXTED BACK: Got it. I'll be
down Friday evening.

May 5, 2016

< Sent BT, LB, MF, and MP
picture of trail from our cabin to
Winton.

< TEXTED: Cinco de Mayo Pub
crawl in Winton!

> MP: Nice!

DELETED

> MP: Fun!

DELETED

> MP: Be there shortly!

< TEXTED BACK: Do not
screw with me.
(He lives in the cities.)

> MP: Oh sure?

DELETED

> MP: I'm taking my dog out.

DELETED

> LB: Haha I was going to say
what does a pub crawl in Winton entail? Moving from the bar
to a table at the Roadhouse?

DELETED

> MR: We better unload that
sofa Friday night then so it's
ready for the movers to haul out

CALLED BACK: He has his
weekends screwed up. Move is
next weekend.

first thing in the morning. Maybe we just leave it somewhere near the lobby overnight! Less doors to maneuver.

< Sent BT, LB, PT, MF, & MP picture sitting at lake shore.
< TEXTED: Back home from cinco de mayo! How do you spell cinco de mayo anyway?

> MF: That's close enough for me. DELETED

> PT: I hope that doesn't mean you are crawling home from the roadhouse. DELETED

> PT: Don't know, don't care! CALLED BACK (Had to check in.)

May 8, 2016
> MR: Happy Mothers' Day to all the mom's on this message. Here is P's new contact info starting May 14th… next Saturday already! SAVED contact info & forwarded it to PT

> SJ: Thank you Happy Mothers' Day! DELETED (Not for me.)

> LR: Same to you. DELETED (Not for me.)

May 9, 2016
> MR: He gets fired on Saturday and hired on Monday. Dave Joeger signed a 3 year $12 million deal with Sacremento. Double what Memphis paid him. DELETED (I get ESPN also.)

> BT: That worked out well for him. DELETED (Not for me.)

May 10, 2016

Another celebrity flip phone user sighting. My wife and I went to the movie tonight and saw Captain America "Civil War." Apparently Captain America has a flip phone according to what I noticed in a scene near the end of the movie. If a flip phone is good enough for Steve Rogers, once again, I feel validated!

May 11, 2016

> JS: When is Region Volleyball this year?

DELETED (I'll call her back later.)

> JS: One week later than normal?

< TEXTED BACK: Nov 4-5

> JS: Thanks, that what I thought. We have a b-ball tourney the next weekend. Then ok got it.

DELETED

> Unknown: Nov. 4&5

DELETED (Probably for JS.)

May 12, 2016

< Sent 4 pictures of cabin to my computer.

May 14, 2016

> MR: Picture of my mom at her new place.

< FORWARDED picture to my computer & message: Your mom is looking pretty relaxed talking to TT on her cell phone.

> TT: I'd say. Her living room looks pretty big.

DELETED (Not for me.)

> SJ: Looks nice.

DELETED (Not for me.)

> MR: I heard the kids have a new car to go with their new driver's permit. Why haven't we seen a picture of the two standing next to it in the beautiful California sunshine?

DELETED (Definitely not for me. I'm fishing on opening day at Fall Lake and it is 29 degrees.)

> TT: Amen!

DELETED (Not for me but maybe it will help the fishing.)

May 15, 2016
> MR: Still waiting for the picture from the west coast.

DELETED (Not for me. I'm fishing on Fall Lake again this morning. It is up to 38 degrees. MR needs to be fishing so I stop getting caught in these group messages.

> AC: Sent picture of small Adirondack chair.

< TEXTED BACK: Looks good! Message: Got this mini chair for BB's birthday.

May 16, 2016
> PM: Camp in Sleepy Eye next week. You have any interest? Striking out all over.

< TEXTED BACK: Projects at the lake.

> PM: I bet. Thanks. Any interest in doing any this summer?

< TEXTED BACK: Top 100!

May 17, 2016
> BT: Sent a list of campgrounds near wedding.

< FORWARDED to BL

> SJ: I received your book. Thank you!!

< TEXTED BACK: I hope you and the kids like it.

> BL: Got it!

May 19, 2016

I think I already knew this, but I was watching the Today Show this morning and Jenna Bush was interviewing Dallas Cowboy owner Jerry Jones and his daughter; at one point, he proudly broke out his flip phone and showed it off. Impressive!

TEXTED JJ: What is your student ID #? I need to check grades. Coach (I had left her a voice message earlier and hadn't

> JJ: I am at work & my wallet is in my car. I'll text it to you when I can.

> JJ: My student ID number is xxxxxxxxx.

heard back.)

< TEXTED BACK: Thanks.

< TEXTED BACK: Thanks. (FORWARDED to MF.)

< Sent BT pictures of his paddleboard I picked up.

> BT: Awesome, thanks!

< TEXTED BACK: Exactly 10 feet.

< Sent BT, MF, & JB picture of Walleye I caught off the dock at the cabin.

> BT: Now that's an eater!

> MF: Nice fish! I'll go in tomorrow and print J's transcripts.

> JB: Nice, jealous!

DELETED

DELETED

DELETED

May 20, 2016

< Sent MF J's cell number.

< TEXTED JJ: Call MF ASAP. Coach

< TEXTED BT: My mom's new phone number is [XXX] XXX-XXXX. (He had called earlier.)

May 21, 2016

> DH: You have to watch this. [Sent link to Gopher baseball team's tribute to pitching coach.]

SAVED

May 23, 2016

> MF: Just wanted to give you a heads up. TR yesterday & let me know that he will be resigning second coaching job if he would extend my annuitant retirement. No golf, way out of offered &

< TEXTED BACK: ?@#* great! I told MR a few weeks ago that I would take on a from all 3 coaching positions after he gets back from the national golf tournament. He was my com-

fort accepted an assistant job at
UW-Stout. If you have any ideas
on how to fill these positions
let me know. I will try to meet
with MR this week after work. I
spoke with him yesterday some.
> MF: What did he say?

> MF: OK, like I said I am going
to try to meet with him later in
the week.

zone!

< TEXTED BACK: Haven't
heard back from him.
< TEXTED BACK: OK, stop
texting me. MR call after work.
(We talked later that night.)

**Great, there goes my retirement plans. Better call my wife
and let her know there might be a snag in the plans.**

< TEXTED JJ: Have you sent
your Saint N transcripts to
MF yet? Coach P.S. The Fax is
[XXX] XXX-XXXX.
< TEXTED SH: I am up for the
Top 100 if needed.

May 24, 2016
> SH: Perfect!
> PH: Hey, do I need a physical
every year for sports?
> PH: Can you email that form
please?
> LR: A few 5th grade teachers
are going to read your book to
their classes. I will try to get
feedback for you. [Followed by 2
empty squares.]

DELETED
< TEXTED BACK: Yes

CALLED BACK

[She doesn't know my phone
doesn't receive emojis.]
< TEXTED BACK: Thanks!
That's great.

May 26, 2016
> LB: Sent video of grandson
walking. Message: Thought I
could get a good video of him

SAVED & FORWARDED to BT
and my computer.

walking but 5:00 usually starts
crabby time.

May 27, 2016

< Sent PT pictures of log siding
on WO building at the lake.

> CV: I took the Mesabi baseball
job!

< TEXTED BACK: Congrats!
< FORWARDED MF & DB
message from CV.

> DB: You did?
> MF: Sure you did!
> CV: Thanks my friend!

DELETED
DELETED
DELETED
< TEXTED MF & DB: I for-
warded that message from CV.

> DB: That's good news!
> MF: Funny, I just texted BS
and told him you were taking
the job. Good for V!
> MF: Yeah, the posting was
emailed out to all faculty & staff
today.

DELETED
< TEXTED BACK: Any word
from MR?

< TEXTED BACK: What did he
say about my offer? SR talked
to me about possibly taking
softball back. We will see what
happens.

> MF: He said he wants to see
what he gets from the posting
first. He wasn't against it though.

< CALLED BACK: I am tired of
this texting nonsense.

**When talking to MF, he explained to me what an idiot I
am. I didn't know when you forward a texted message
it appears as if it came straight from you. The receiver
doesn't see who you received the message from. I always
thought it worked like email. Left me wondering how
many other rumors I have started by forwarding texts? I
hope nobody thinks I took the Mesabi job; CV did and it is
his dream job.**

May 28, 2016

< TEXTED LB: Please forward BB video to my computer.

May 30, 2016

< Sent BT & AC pictures of B on his paddleboard.

> AC: Very cool! Can't wait to try it!

< TEXTED BACK: These are all BT.

> AC: Did you give it a whirl?

< TEXTED BACK: No

> TC: You're coming tomorrow?

< TEXTED BACK: Yes, I already talked to RP.

> TC: Perfect!

DELETED

May 31, 2016

> RP: Cancelled today, rescheduled tomorrow.

< TEXTED BACK: Same times?

> RP: Yes

DELETED

> TC: I need an address for you so we can write a check for working tomorrow.

< TEXTED BACK: XXXX Xth Ave E XXXXXXX, MN XXXXX

> TC: Thanks. We will pay you $100 for the day. Press box and working on the field between games.

DELETED

< Sent BT, MF, LB, and my computer some cabin pictures.

> LB: Looks like B will have an awesome fishing guide when he comes up!

DELETED

> MF: Too bad you didn't get ten of those. Nice fish!

DELETED

June 1, 2016

> BT: Pictures of Navy Pier in Chicago, taken from his hotel window.

< TEXTED BACK: To steal a line from A, very cool!

< Sent PT, LB, BT, and my computer picture of rainbow over

Fall Lake. MESSAGE: I don't
know if you can see the rainbow
out there or not.

Another reason for my opposition to smart phones: My
wife and I were at Lowe's the other day. We went to the
garden center and bought 30 landscaping wall blocks and
16 bags of mulch. The lady at the counter asked if I wanted
help loading out. I said, "No." My wife went into the store
to buy other items while I loaded our pick-up truck. The
kid working outside the garden center in the loading area
spent the next half hour watching me loading the truck
while he thumbed through who knows what on his cell
phone. He never offered to help me.

I blame lack of self-initiative and being too distracted by
his phone. May not have happened if he had a flip phone.
My wife reminded me that I told the lady at the counter
that I did not need help loading out. I'm sticking with
my theory, because I don't think that kid had any way of
knowing that. Unless the lady at the counter had texted
him that information.

June 3, 2016
> TR: Did you hear about M?   CALLED BACK (M is one of
                                                   my players and for some reason,
                                                   I feel like this isn't good news.)

I was right. This wasn't good news—actually, it was tragic!
TR didn't have all the details so I had to call another player
to find out what was really going on. This might be me, but
I really think there is something innately wrong with de-
livering or hinting at bad news in a text message. At least
call if speaking directly to the person is not possible. Does
our thumb disconnect from our brain, our heart, and our
emotions when sending a text message? I hope to hell they
don't come up with an emoji for bad news! For all I know,
somebody already has and there are social misfits using it.

June 4, 2016

> LB: Sent pictures of grand-son at the farm pretending to drive equipment.

SAVED & TEXTED BACK: Farmer's permit?

> LB: Haha, yep! They start them young in Nebraska.

DELETED

Keep in mind, my grandson is 11 months old.

June 5, 2016

< TEXTED JJ: Have you checked your eligibility with MF yet? Summer session starts June 6 (tomorrow). Coach T

> MF: B's cell number is [XXX] XXX-XXXX. I haven't seen anything from JJ. I was just at my office on Thurs-day.

I had called him yesterday to get B's cell number and ask about JJ.
< TEXTED BACK: Thanks, sorry to bug you last night, forgot about graduation.

> MF: Not a problem.

< Sent MF picture of my grandson sitting on the trac-tor. MESSAGE: My grandson the farmer. They issue the permits early in Nebraska.

> MF: Cute!

DELETED
< Sent PT, LB, BT, KB, & JR picture of another rainbow over Fall Lake.

> BT: Another one?

DELETED

> PT: Nice!

DELETED

June 6, 2016

> LB: Sent pictures of grand-son.

FORWARDED to my com-puter.

June 7, 2016
> JJ: I just emailed them to   CALLED BACK
you. I just got them.

June 8, 2016
> MF: I got your message.   < TEXTED BACK: Just let
I've been working long   me know when you have her
hours & haven't been to the   eligibility figured out.
college since last week some-
time. Not sure if I'll get there
until this weekend.

June 10, 2016
> LB: Sent pictures of grand-   FORWARDED to my com-
son.   puter.
> LB: Sent more pictures of   FORWARDED to my com-
my grandson trying on his   puter.
tuxedo for my son's wed-   < TEXTED BACK: Just like
ding.   his grandpa Mike! MES-
    SAGE: Too hot, doesn't want
    clothes on. Should work,
    pants a little long.

> PT: What size is it? Should   DELETED (Not for me.)
it be next size?
> PT: We need to get him to   DELETED (Not for me.)
Minnesota, where it is cooler.
He is going to be so hand-
some! Should I bring needle
& thread?
> LB: No because the jacket   DELETED (Not for me.)
and vest fits good. Better
bring needle and thread just
in case.
> LB: Two blank squares.   DELETED (Emojis I can't
    receive.)

**My son's wedding is June 25th. I'm sure I'll be receiving
more texts not for me in the next week and a half.**

June 11, 2016

> BT: Is there a cover for the canopy?
> MF: I got JJ's transcripts. She has 19 credits. I still don't know about FDL yet.

> PT: Way to go dear! Are you grilling them on Sunday for our anniversary dinner?
> JB: When do you plan on coming down to the CWS?

> SH: Nice!
> JL: Picture of Walleye filets. MESSAGE: Dinner at Bowstring!
> BS: Picture of a bottle of Coors Light. MESSAGE: Dinner at the Roosevelt Bar!

June 12, 2016
> JJ: How many credits is it for full time again?
> JJ: Thanks

< Sent PT and my computer pictures of Ravens at the lake. MESSAGE: Bob?

< Sent BT & PT pictures of Boat Lift I looked at today.
< TEXTED BACK: Yes

< CALLED BACK

< Sent several people pictures of some big crappies I caught on Fall Lake. MESSAGE: Dinner at Fall Lake!

< CALLED BACK: We'll grill them at home tonight.

< CALLED BACK: great news, the Testicle Festival is the day before the College World Series and I'll be there.
DELETED
< TEXTED BACK: Nice!

< TEXTED BACK: It is better with fish!

< TEXTED BACK: 12 credits per semester.

< CALLED BACK: Making sure she got registered.

June 13, 2016

I heard on the radio today that waitresses/waiters are claiming that people using their cell phones are costing them money. Customers spend time looking at their phones and don't look at the menu right away. Also people are spending time on their phones and it takes them longer to eat. These waitresses/waiters it costs them at least two tables a shift.

Restaurants, on the other hand, like the publicity they get from customers posting pictures of their food on Instagram. I don't affect either, I usually leave my flip phone in my truck when I go into eat. I eat fairly fast and always tip 20%, but I do not participate on Instagram or any other social media on my phone. I will admit to having a Linked In account on my computer.

June 15, 2016

> LB: Sent picture of grandson.

SAVED

< TEXTED MF: Any word on JJ or job postings yet?

> MF: No & no. Tried to get in touch with MR today but he never called me back.

< TEXTED BACK: [00] That is what I sent and I don't know how.
< TEXTED BACK: OK, that was my emoji for, "I can't text."

> MF: Nice!

< TEXTED BACK: Glad you are on top of things!

> MF: I was at school last night & I didn't have an email from JJ either.

< TEXTED BACK: Go pave something!

< TEXTED JJ: Did you get those FDL transcripts yet?

> MF: Too wet to pave today. Hauled lots of Winton Point road.

< TEXTED BACK: Bring some to XXX crushed rock today though.

June 17, 2016

< Sent BT the phone number for where my mom is. Started trying to text her but she called before I was done.

> SJ: How is mom doing today?
> AT&T: Number for North Memorial hospital [XXX] XXX-XXXX.
> TT: Mike's cell: [XXX] XXX-XXXX.

DELETED (I had called directory assistance to confirm the number.)
DELETED (I am Mike.)

My mom was put in the hospital last night. My sister and I left there at 3:00 AM this morning. She should be fine. I had to leave at 8:30 AM to go to Omaha for the College World Series and to see my daughter, son-in-law, and grandson.

< Sent a bunch of people pictures from dinner at the Testicle Festival in Ashland, NE. MESSAGE: They are chewy!

> CV: Yum! DELETED
> CV: Ha Ha! DELETED
> SH: The Silver Fox! DELETED
> BS: I'm not sure what to think of this? DELETED

< Sent more pictures from the Testicle Festival. MESSAGE: Bucket list, check!

> LU: Ah, where is the fox? DELETED

> BT: Dave is coming to the CWS TUE-THU

< CALLED BACK

> LR: Notes on Mom; PT & doctor recommend a few days of rehab. I will drive her to Austin on Monday. T says there will be a bed there. Doctor will be back to talk soon. Blood tests will not be complete until Saturday. She does have an infection. Thanks to A for visiting and bringing nice gifts.

< CALLED BACK

> MF: How did they taste?

< TEXTED BACK: Like chicken!

> MJ: Careful you might be walking into something you don't expect.

DELETED

> LB: Awesome!

DELETED

> LR: Labs are back. Blood infection… not good. Will continue antibiotics. Doctor and infectious disease specialist will consult tomorrow. Call nurse tomorrow. B will go there in morning. M & I are leaving for Milwaukee in the morning. Grandchildren unite.

< CALLED BACK

> BT: Thanks for the update.

DELETED (Not for me.)

> JM: No wonder our wives don't like them. I didn't say that F; stole my phone.

DELETED

> SJ: Do you know what time doctors are consulting?

DELETED (Not for me.)

> SJ: I talked to Mom and she did not know.

DELETED (Not for me.)

> MR: You never know when a doctor will show it is a waiting game. DELETED (Not for me.)

> MR: Why is the time a concern? DELETED (Not for me.)

I am really glad all these people are not on the same group message. These are two totally different topics.

> Sent LR some pictures from the Testicle Festival to lighten her mood. DELETED (Not for me.)

> SJ: I was hoping someone could be with Mom. I think they make the rounds in the morning.

> LR: We are leaving at 6:00 AM. DELETED (Not for me.)

> SJ: Someone else? DELETED (Not for me.)

> BR: I will be there tomorrow but can't go until early afternoon. If you can find what time they are consulting, I'll make it work. DELETED (Not for me.)

> SJ: Thanks B. DELETED (Not for me.)

> LR: It is fine B. DELETED (Not for me.)

> TT: Blood infection can be serious/is serious. I am so thankful Mom is in the hospital with infectious disease specialist. All said, I am even more thankful that God is hearing our prayers and is working mightily on mom's behalf. God's peace, love, and comfort to all of you. DELETED

June 18, 2016

< Sent DK picture outside of Happy Bar in Omaha. MESSAGE: Tuesday?

> BR: Nana is doing a lot better today. She is very with it and being herself. Still has a lot of back pain. There is a second blood test tonight. Might be able to switch to pill antibiotic and go to rehab on Monday.

< TEXTED BACK: Great news, thanks!

> TT: Great!

DELETED (Not for me.)

> PT: Good news! B thanks for update and being there.

DELETED (Not for me.)

> BT: Thanks for the update B, good to hear that.

DELETED (Not for me.)

> TT: Thanks for spending a lot of time with Nana.

DELETED (Not for me.)

> BR: Yep, not a problem.

DELETED (Not for me.)

> BR: No problem!

DELETED

> LB: Thanks for everything B, so glad she is doing better.

DELETED (Not for me.)

June 19, 2016

< Sent PT pictures of our grandson.

> AC: Happy Father's Day! Can't wait to be a T. Couldn't ask for a better father-in-law. Hope you have a great day.

< TEXTED BACK: Thanks, this is how my day started. We are all looking forward to you joining the family also. (Sent pictures of feeding grandson.)

> AC: Oh cute! What a great way to start the day. Tell everyone hi and happy father's day to J.

DELETED (Forgot to tell J.)

< Sent pictures of my grand-
son to my computer.
< TEXTED MF: Any word on
coaching positions?
< CALLED BACK (I had al-
ready spoken with my mom.

> LR: I just got off the phone
with mom's nurse. Mom is
in a lot of pain. Nurse said
she moans and screams and
seems confused. Won't get
out until at least Tuesday.
> BT: I will be stopping at
the hospital too.
> LR: Great, thanks!
> TT: My heart goes out to
her. Lifting prayers.
> MF: Talked to R Friday
and he was going to have S
set up interviews.
> LB: I'm headed to bed. The
side door is open. Just lock it
behind you. Hope you had a
good day.

DELETED (Called B.)

DELETED (Not for me.)
DELETED

< TEXTED BACK: I'll be in
Hibbing on Wednesday.

< TEXTED BACK: I'll set my
alarm for 6:30. (I get to watch
my grandson in the morn-
ing.) I need to leave around
7:15 AM, so I'll probably
have to get you up.

June 20, 2016

< Sent PT pictures of our
grandson in his crib in the
morning. MESSAGE: Grand-
pa is babysitting today!
< CALLED BACK

> PT: Does he have to stay in
his crib all day?
> LB: Sent picture of grand-
son. MESSAGE: Grandpa
must have dressed me, dia-
per and onesie are on back-
wards. LOL

< FORWARDED to comput-
er; TEXTED BACK: Let's just
all stop picking on Grandpa
Mike.

> LB: I didn't say it. That came from daycare. I was impressed you were still standing after 4 hours.
> LB: OK perfect. T can't make it, so that is perfect.

< TEXTED BACK: I saved 3 tickets to CWS.

DELETED

< Sent LB picture of TD America Ball Field covered by tarp. MESSAGE: Might be late!
DELETED (I'll call later.)
< Sent LB another picture of rain delay at CWS. MESSAGE: 7:30 start?

> LB: Geez, we just got to Bellevue. Sunny and hot; did it stop raining? Just let me know when you are coming back.
> LR: Just talked to nurse, Mom should have bed at rehab starting Tuesday or Wednesday. Covered by insurance. CAT scan on stomach 5:15 tonight.

< CALLED BACK (My mom is not doing very well. I am leaving Omaha tomorrow.)

> MR: Are you at games tonight? Did you run into GD there?
> MR: Bummer!

< TEXTED BACK: I left after 3 hour rain delay, no.

< Sent PT another picture of our grandson.

Don't get the impression I have converted to a texter; I'm at the College World Series in Omaha and staying with my daughter's family in Auburn. I can't hear my phone in the stadium and service is hit and miss. There is a lot going on, my mom is in the hospital, and my son and AC are getting married this Saturday the 25th. I'll be driving back to Hibbing tomorrow, and will stop and see my mom in Minneapolis on my way back. My wife and I are leaving for the wedding on Thursday. I can't wait to get home and stop this texting hysteria.

June 21, 2016

> JJ: Talked to DP from FDL & he said I have 20 credits from there.

< TEXTED BACK: That's great! I will forward this to MF.

< FORWARDED MF text from JJ

> LR: There is room at Trillium Woods. Still waiting on okay from infectious disease people to OK antibiotics so mom can leave today. I will keep you posted. Mom went to PT today.

< CALLED BACK: I'm on my way back from Omaha; I will stop tonight to see Mom.

> TT: I hope it is not a long wait and the OK comes.

DELETED (Not for me.)

> AC: Once she gets to TW it will be a very busy 24 hours for her with checking in. She will be tired.

DELETED (Not for me.)

> TT: Very true.

DELETED (Not for me.)

> LR: Good news, I can bust her out of here at 3:30, pills okayed. She is excited to get a shower and put some real clothes on.

DELETED

> TT: Great news!

DELETED (Not for me.)

> AC: Let me know when you get to TW, I will

DELETED (Not for me.) try to stop in and see her.

> LR: Don't worry about that you have a lot going

DELETED (Not for me.) on this week. The nurses say if she gets stronger she may get a day pass for the wedding.

> AC: I will be stopping if it works out.

DELETED (Not for me.)

> LR: Okay if it doesn't work, you have MANY things to do.

DELETED (Not for me.)

> LR: Contact information for Trillium the Birches.	SAVED
> AC: When is a good time to call her?	DELETED (Not for me.)
> LR: Anytime, we are done with paperwork for tonight.	DELETED (Not for me.)
	< TEXTED MJ: Did you take the job?
> MJ: I did!	< TEXTED BACK: Congrats!
> MJ: Thank you.	DELETED
	< FORWARDED contact info for my mom to LB.

I got to Minneapolis and visited with my mom for a few hours. Saw my sister briefly in the hallway; she had to go with her daughter and get their manicures for the wedding. Got back to Hibbing around 1:00 AM. Side note: My mom also has a heart condition.

June 22, 2016

> DK: Did you make it to the Happy Bar? I got in	< TEXTED BACK: I am in Hibbing again. too late, but went to the Florida & Texas Tech game.
> LR: Mom did PT 2X today. She is very weak and worn out. Back pain seems a little better. PT says we should all encourage her to drink water etc… Mom is still a bit confused but better. Nurses still say it is infection induced. This is a nice place, but her doctor calls it PT Boot Camp. We all need to encourage her to work hard and rest in between sessions. Her insurance will cover 100% for 100	DELETED (I will call my mom.)

days. Pray for speedy recovery.

> LR: She will be going to dinner at 5:00. She is not happy with her table guests. She told the aide one of the ladies didn't have a brain in her head.	DELETED (Called Mom after dinner.)
> LR: Say anything to her and she gets mad. I am trying to be patient.	DELETED
> LR: T are you heading here on Friday? We are heading to wedding rehearsal dinner on Friday.	DELETED (Not for me)
> TT: I will be there Friday. Spend day with Mom and leave for wedding on Saturday.	DELETED (Not for me)
> LR: Great! Some miracle will have to happen for mom to make it to the wedding. She could not sit that long. We are eating right now.	DELETED (Not for me. I will call LR after I talk to my mom.)
> TT: L, let's talk tomorrow; keys, directions, etc…	DELETED (Not for me.)
> LR: OK	DELETED (Not for me.)
> JJ: We can start the season on the 5th correct? Brainerd the 18th? Trying to pick a start date.	< CALLED BACK (I can never keep pace with her texting.)

You may have noticed that SJ has been missing from the communication lately. She and her family are flying out from California for the wedding and were hoping to see our mom first. They have been stuck in the Chicago airport for 24 hours. Hopefully they will get to Minneapolis late tonight.

I hope my son and daughter-in-law to be are dealing with all of this okay; the wedding is in two days. My wife's mom and dad are also in poor health and they are doing everything in their power to get from Ely to Glenwood for the wedding. One way or the other, it is all going to happen.

My wife and I leave tomorrow and my daughter, grandson, and son-in-law will be driving up from Nebraska. It will be our grandson's first birthday.

Tonight, I will pray for a great day and improved health for our parents. I am glad God doesn't request text messages or have a Facebook or Twitter account!

June 26, 2016

> LR: B and I are leaving the hotel in 10 minutes. — DELETED (Not for me.)

> PT: We are just heading out. We should be in 10 minutes. We can stop at the hotel. — DELETED (Not for me. I am with PT.)

> LR: Yes! Great. We will meet you at the front doors. — DELETED (Not for me.)

> LR: We are at the Grand Stay hotel. — DELETED (Not for me.)

> LR: We dropped the tux off no problem. — DELETED (Not for me.)

June 27, 2016

> SJ: What is the name of the AF Academy hockey coach that you know? There is a hockey camp going on here also. — < CALLED BACK

B & A's wedding was great. We had three fabulous days in Glenwood. The only down note is that my mom couldn't get out of the hospital to attend the wedding. P's mom and dad made it. We are heading up to the lake now for the 4th of July weekend. Hopefully the only texts I get are forwarded pictures from the wedding. Side note: June 23–25th were great, no text messaging right before, during, or after the wedding. Welcomed relief!

> KB: I'm sorry, was on the phone with P. Happy Holiday!

DELETED (I told her Happy 4th when I was leaving the office.)

June 29, 2016
> SJ: We found F at the AF Academy!

< TEXTED BACK: No charge for the entertainment!

> BM: Hey Mike, this is BM. Just wanted to contact you so you have my number. Look forward to working with you and the rest of the staff. Take care!

< TEXTED BACK: Congrats on the new job. Welcome, let me know whenever I can help you.
(Brad is our new men's basketball coach. I will be able to retire In May of 2017.)

> LB: Sent picture of deer eating out of my birdfeeder at the cabin.

< TEXTED BACK: That is not a deer feeder!

June 30, 2016
Today is the last day of June and will be the last day I log text messages into this book. I am hoping to receive no text messages or send any. That would make for a great day!

I got through June 30th, but it was a short-lived reprieve. My sisters rattled off 12 straight group texts on July 1st, wishing the family a Happy Fourth of July weekend. I responded by sending out a picture of a campfire at the lake and telling everyone to stop texting and relax!

Let's sum up the past two months:

MAY 1–JUNE 30 2016

194	INCOMING TEXTS
50	MESSAGES NOT FOR ME [25%]
19	CALLED BACK [9%]
106	DELETED RIGHT AWAY [54%]
8	FORWARDED MESSAGE [4%]
4	SAVED [2%]
44	*TEXTED BACK [22%]
23	I SENT A PICTURE
14	**I SENT ORIGINAL TEXT

* Shame on me!
** That is 7 per month.

COMPARING MAR–APR TO MAY–JUN

INCOMING TEXTS [Up 68; Brutal!]
MESSAGES NOT FOR ME [Up 25/6%]
(I have to get off those group messages.)
CALLED BACK [Up 6/-1% of messages]
DELETED RIGHT AWAY [Up 37/% Same]
FORWARDED MESSAGE [Up 8/4%]
SAVED [Down 10/9%]
TEXTED BACK [Up 27/8%] (People I need to train.)
I SENT A PICTURE [Down 2]
I SENT ORIGINAL TEXT [Up 13] (Oh, the shame!)

TOTALS JUNE 25 2015– JUNE 30 2016

(TOTAL DAYS: 372/1 Year and 7 days)

621	INCOMING TEXT MESSAGES
111	MESSAGES NOT FOR ME [18%]
96	CALLED BACK [15%]
307	DELETED RIGHT AWAY [49%]
12	FORWARDED MESSAGE [1%]
52	SAVED [8%]
119	TEXTED BACK [19%]
70	I SENT A PICTURE
37	I SENT ORIGINAL TEXT MESSAGE

* Mostly pictures of grandson

SUB TOTALS

64	SAVED or FORWARDED MESSAGE [10%]
215	CALLED BACK or TEXTED BACK [34%]
307	DELETED RIGHT AWAY [49%]
107	I SENT PICTURE or ORIGINAL TEXT MESSAGE
621	INCOMING TEXT MESSAGES
238	OUTGOING MESSAGING

-383 (+ 383 in my world)

BREAKDOWN

119	TEXTED BACK
12	FORWARDED MESSAGE
70	SENT PICTURE
37	SENT ORIGINAL TEXT
238	TOTAL

AVERAGES PER DAY

1.66	INCOMING TEXT MESSAGES
.29	MESSAGES NOT FOR ME
.25	CALLED BACK
.82	DELETED RIGHT AWAY
.03	FORWARDED MESSAGE
.13	SAVED MESSAGE
.31	TEXTED BACK
.18	I SENT A PICTURE
.09	I SENT ORIGINAL TEXT MESSAGE
1.66	INCOMING TEXT MESSAGES
.63	OUTGOING MESSAGING

IN CONCLUSION

This unofficial experiment started on June 25, 2015, and ended on June 30, 2016. As you read through the messages and the final numbers, please keep in mind that I was 56 years old when I started and was 57 years old by the time the accounts came to a close.

I said in the beginning that I would trade in my flip phone for a smart phone if the numbers showed a pending reason to do so. I am proud to say my flip phone is still working and I will continue to use it until it no longer works or I lose it.

What I require from my cell phone is relatively simple. 1] Make and receive phone calls. 2] Receive text messages. 3] In a real pinch, send a rare text message. 4] Receive voicemails. 5] Take and receive pictures. My flip phone still allows me to do these things, so despite the mounting peer pressure, I am sticking with it.

Most of the people in my life realize that I do not find any joy or ease in texting and attempt to contact me by calling, leaving voicemails, or emailing me. Because of this, I feel I enjoy a much more personal relationship with the people I need to communicate with.

I will admit that I like to receive or send the occasional picture. My flip phone allows me to do that, so it is all good.

I am guessing that the vast majority of you will find that my use of a cell phone is way below your own personal use and national averages. As I said before, I receive a sense of joy when I open my phone and the RECENT CALLS screen reads: NO CALL LOG. When I go on and check my INBOX and it reads: EMPTY, I become giddy. I feel a deep sense of pride when I check MESSAGES SENT and it reads: EMPTY. On the other hand, I become somewhat stressed when I open my phone and discover several incoming messages. That stress level elevates when I realize that I will probably have to text back or the only way to get a message to someone is to text them.

I realize that if this book is published that AT&T, Verizon, Samsung, Apple, T-Mobile, Sprint, or any other such businesses will probably not be calling on me to do any endorsements anytime soon. If anyone has an app for automatically shutting your phone off at 10:00 PM or eliminating messages not pertaining to you, I will gladly endorse those.

I have heard several people say, "I don't know what we did without cell phones." I am not exactly sure how old you have to be to know the answer to that, but I am. I miss phone booths, rotary dial phones, phone cards, land lines, and even party lines. If you do not know these terms, ask Google or take the time to let someone who does remember these things tell you about them. We are still out there and would love to impart the knowledge on you.

I will continue to progress through this wonderful life with my flip phone in hand for as long as I can. If you are also a flip phone user, don't hide the fact; be proud, remain calm, and soldier on. Know that there are more of us out there and you are still loved!

If you are not a flip phone user and find that the only way your phone can be removed from you is through some kind of surgery, seriously consider putting the phone down and looking up. There is a whole world out there that may be passing you by.

Start slow—baby steps! Try going to a game or a movie and actually watching it. Go to a restaurant and talk to the people who are sitting at your table. The next time you really want to send a text, call someone and talk to them. If you really want to try something bold, write a letter. If you are a student, try shutting your phone off when you are in class. Tonight, when you go to bed, shut your phone off and don't turn it on until tomorrow morning. Once you get over the shakes, you will probably notice how rested you are.

When I finished writing this book, I was asked, "What is your number one reason for wanting to keep your flip phone?" I have thought long and hard about this. The answer is: My grandson, who is one, loves the Ch-Ch sound my phone makes when I take his picture! My own children who are 33 and 31 are embarrassed by the same sound!

AND I WEAR SKINNY JEANS

I would be remiss if I did not come back to this. After reading this book, you might have been wondering where this would come into play. In recording my text activity throughout the year, I discovered many things about my life that I had not really taken note of. I already knew that I did not like skinny jeans but I do wear them. My jeans of choice are Wrangler Relaxed Fit and I occasionally splurge on Levi's. Despite my skinny legs, I spend as much of the year as I can in shorts and sweats. When I am not wearing those, I prefer jeans.

My weight tends to fluctuate throughout the year. In the winter months, my jeans tend to fit snugger. When I wear them in the summer and fall and my weight is down, those same jeans tend to fall off my butt and I need to create more holes in my belt. Instead of breaking down and getting suspenders, I just call those same jeans my "Skinny Jeans."

OCTOBER 30, 2016:
"Thinking Out Loud" By, Mike Turnbull

My Hibbing CC Volleyball team lost at Central Lakes College yesterday ending our 2016 season.

I woke up this morning crabby, somewhat lost and slightly depressed; as I usually am at the end of any season, good or bad.

This year it feels a little different though, I realized that after 36 years of coaching this was my last season. I will be officially retired in May of 2017, but for all practical purposes this was my last season of coaching. I'm dealing with that thought okay, but it hit me that for the first time since the fall of 1981 I do not have a team to coach. Later, as I was raking leaves, I consoled myself with the thought that I now have one big team. 76 teams over 36 years; baseball, basketball, volleyball [High school & college/men's and women's teams]. Along with several teams that I served as an assistant coach. That roughs out to about 2,000 ex-players. How blessed can one guy be?

I can't really put into words how grateful and thankful I am to have had the career I have had, but I will try. I do realize I am truly blessed and humbled to have had all of you in my life and now cherished memories.

THANK YOUS!

Thanks to my Uncle Gene Soltner, long-time Football & Track coach at Eddystone & Ridley Park in Pennsylvania, for introducing me to coaching at an early age. Gene Halvorson & Tery Teiken for giving me the opportunity to coach & teach at Lake Park high school 36 years ago. Jim Sundstrom and Lowell Roisum for granting me the same opportunity at Wadena high school. Al Holmes and Sally Ihne for believing in me enough to hire me for my first college coaching job at Brainerd CC [Central Lakes College] 24 years ago. Anna Van-Tassel & Tony Kuznik for hiring me at Hibbing CC 20 years ago. Gerry Levos for talking me in to trading out classes for her volleyball coaching job, supposedly for one year, 17 years ago. Also thanks to the people that were responsible for my hiring at Norwood-Young America & Ely high schools. I hope I did all of you proud.

I would be remiss if I didn't thank the countless people who didn't hire me for other jobs I applied for. I realize in some twisted form of fate you all helped guide me on the special journey I had.

Most importantly, thanks to my wife, Pam & kids [Lexie & Blaine] for allowing me to chase my dreams, coach and drag you all over the state. Nobody will ever really understand how much give and take that goes on in a coach's family unless they live that life.

INFLUENCES & MENTORS

My Mom: Taught me to be passionate about sports and everything you hold dear in your life.

My Dad: Taught me to remember sports are just a game.

The following people that I have either coached with, for or against have all impacted my career along the way. The common threads are passion, dignity, integrity, commitment and team first mentalities.

Terrel Harrison, Coach Grant, Len Nardone, George Marsnik, Larry Mischke, Bob Altuvilla, Bob Montibello, Bud Ode, Blacky Variano, Paul Weinzerl, John Paulson, Denny Kaatz, Fred Pollack, Whitey Aus, Denny Anderson, Jef McCarron, Jane Peterson, Al Holmes, Denny Eastman, Art Westphal, Bill Wirtanen, Dave Retzlaff, Tom Tintor, Bob & Paul McDonald, Tom Stackpool, Chris Vito, Rick Tintor, Dan Bergan, Julie Lange, Anna VanTassel, Gerry Levos, Julie Lange, Mike Flaten, Kurt Zuidmulder, Murray Anderson, Matt Johnson, Dave Bevacqua, Kate Brau, Ken Miller & Mel Millerbernd.

I have to add Coach John Wooden to this list. I always idolized Coach Wooden from afar and I will always be grateful to John Potter for arranging the opportunity to talk to Coach Wooden on the phone. We had about a half hour conversation. I asked him when he speaks to kids what the number one thing is he tells them? He said, "the same thing I tell adults, we all have things to say and knowledge to share, slow down and take the time to listen to each other."

TWO TEAMS I WANT TO SPECIALLY THANK

In the 36 years I coached, I never missed a practice or a game and I'm very proud of that. Twice in my career I almost did, but two teams in particular helped me through some very tough times. The two toughest times in my career to blend my life with coaching is when my father died on New Year's Day in 1989 and this past September when my mom passed away. I want my 1988-89 boys' basketball team in Wadena and this year's Cardinal Volleyball team to know how important a role you played in helping me navigate through some extremely tough days. You helped in ways you'll never really know. That is what families do and I have always considered my teams an extension of my family.

GOOD & BAD CHANGES OVER THE YEARS

No particular order, you can decide which are good or bad or possibly just change for the sake of change.

~ At one time we traveled with CB radios or Walkie-Talkies.

~ Players played cards, Game Boys, or Walk-Mans on the bus.

~ Use to never worry about academic eligibility with female players.

~ Three Point Shot

~ Three person referee crews. [Kept Babe's career going]

~ 16 mm film, video tape, DVD's, streaming, HUDL

~ Shot Clock

~ Rally scoring in Volleyball

~ Volleyball Sets: 25 points instead of 30 points.

~ 3 out of 5 instead of 2 out of 3

~ Smaller bat barrels

~ Flat laces on baseballs

~ Basketball: Longer shorts

~ Meal money for a weekend trip went from $12 to $60

~ Volleyball players wore basketball uniforms, then "Bunzers", then baggy shorts and now spandex.

~ Uniforms: Wool, polyester, nylon, dry weave

~ Charter buses

~ Dittos, Overheads, Computers, Lap-Tops, I-Pads

~ Land-lines, flip phones [that's it I still have one]

~ Quarters went to halves

~ I couldn't use a computer [still hate them] now I kind of can and I have written 5 books. I also type my daily practice schedules and recommendation letters.

~ Somewhere between 1981 & 2016 I went from being MR T to COACH T!

~ Soon I'll just be the OLD CREEPY GUY at the end of the road.

In closing, I just want to reach out and thank every student-athlete I was ever blessed to have the opportunity to Coach and/or teach. Whether you were a Parker, Timberwolf, Indian, Wolverine, Raider or Cardinal; you all share a very special place in my heart and most cherished memories. I'm still trying to get my head wrapped around the fact that I have ex-players that are 18 to 53 years old. All you senior citizens please know that I refer to you as kids when I'm sharing stories about you.

If this [I guess, I'll call it a testimony] finds its' way to you please share it with others. I don't do Facebook, so don't look for me there, but feel free to post, tweet or whatever it is you do with this stuff.

Just know that I am doing very well, looking forward to the next phase in my life. I truly hope all of you and yours are doing well also. If you ever get the chance, do stop by at the end of the road at Fall Lake and we can visit. Pam and I will be moving there, permanently after we sell our Bed & Breakfast in Hibbing.

Humbly Submitted by, Mike Turnbull November 1, 2016

Mike Turnbull

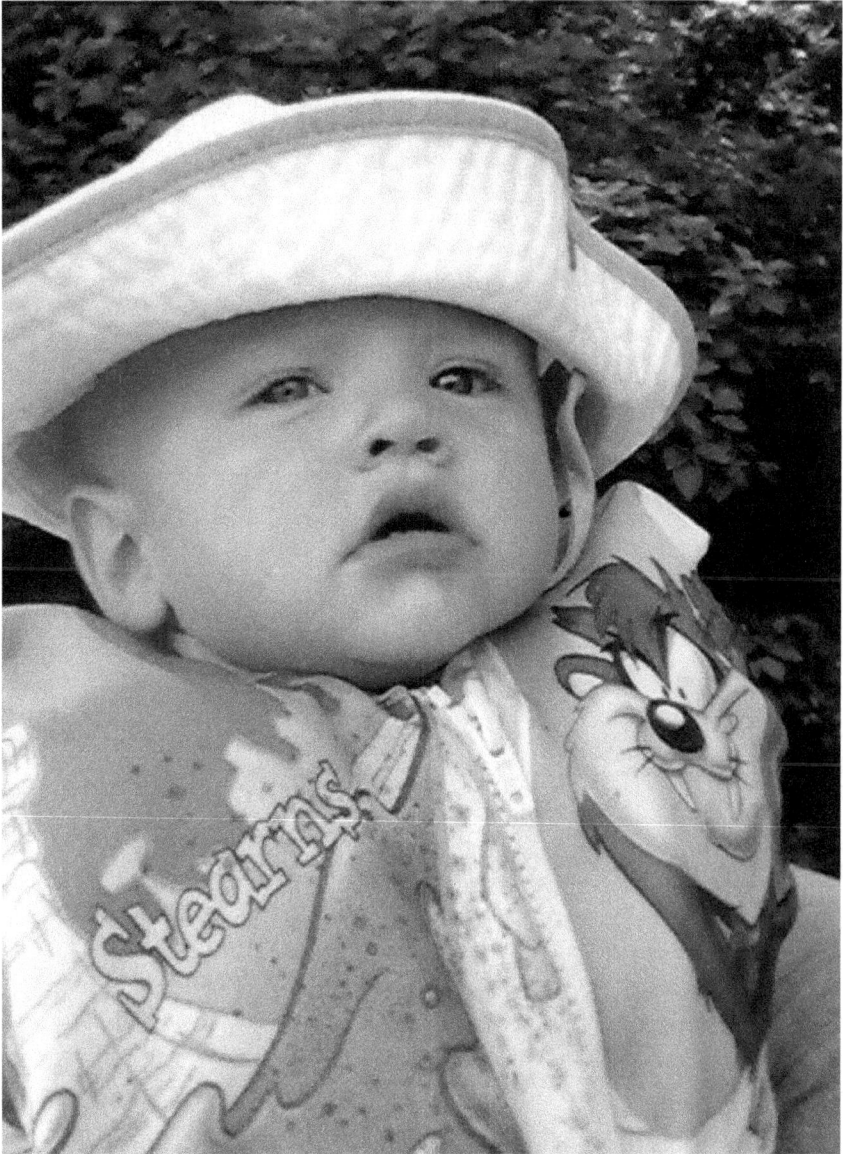

ABOUT THE AUTHOR

I am 57 years old and my wife and I are going on our 35th year of marriage. Pam and I have lived in Hibbing for the past 20 years. I coach and teach at Hibbing Community College and Pam runs the Mitchell-Tappan House Bed and Breakfast in Hibbing. Pam and I own and live in the B&B, but she is the Innkeeper and I claim to be "The Charming" Groundskeeper. Either way, she is the boss and does a great job. Come stay with us sometime; better yet, buy the place. I hope to be officially retired in May of 2017 and we have the B&B up for sale. When we sell, we hope to move to our cabin on Fall Lake outside of Winton, MN.

Pam and I have two grown children. Our daughter Lexie and her husband Jeff live in Auburn, NE, and they have one son, Beckett. Our son Blaine and his wife Alex live in the Minneapolis area and were married this past June.

Pam and I are very excited as we enter this next phase of our life. We now have two married children, one grandson, and hopefully more grandchildren coming in the near future. We have enjoyed having the B&B since 2004 but look forward to other ventures. I have taught and coached all over Minnesota for the past 36 years. I say I am retiring in May of 2017, but I suspect that may be short lived. Either way, I am looking forward to cutting back and seeing what happens next. We hope to be able to spend more time in Nebraska so we can see more of our grandson without stressing out Lexie and Jeff too much.

We both look forward to spending a lot more time at the lake. We have a beautiful place up there and have already done a lot of work on the place and look forward to future remodeling.

I wrote my first book in 2012, and I Still Own a Flip Phone is my fifth. I am humbled to have been blessed to be able to share these books with you and I hope you enjoy reading them as much as I have enjoyed writing them. I am thankful that Rivershore Books has agreed to publish my fifth book and I look forward to working with them in the future. I don't really know at this point where my warped mind may lead me, but whenever the light goes on again, I will be sure to write it down.

I have always taken pride in being referred to as "Coach" second to my favorite titles of "Husband," "Dad," and "Grandpa Mike." I still am humbled when I see "Author" in front of my name. I am still hoping this will help me gain entry into the "Stupid Man" club, if and when I get to heaven.

"I Still Own A Flip Phone"

~ And I Wear Skinny Jeans ~

Mike Turnbull July 11, 2016

AFTERWORD

September 16, 2016: My mom passed away yesterday. My sister and other members of my family have been exchanging text messages for the last couple of months, updates about my mom's condition and health status. It was extremely tough this morning; I woke up and turned on my phone, expecting to check updates as usual and it hit me: no updates.

October 30, 2016: Crisis averted! My flip phone went on the fritz on Friday. The screen kept blanking out all weekend. Charged it up, but that didn't help. Sunday on the way back from the lake I stopped in the new AT&T store in Virginia. They gave me a number and about an hour later one of the workers was able to help me. I told her right away that if they couldn't fix it, I wanted a new flip phone. She lamented but managed to find one in the back. So, I am the proud owner of a new flip phone.

November 2, 2016: Today was/is my mom's birthday. Spent a lot of time thinking about her. At some point in the day I ended up removing her name and information from my contact list. She is and always will be in a much more important contact list. She is etched in my thoughts, memories, prayers, and heart.

BOOKS BY
MIKE TURNBULL

*All the books are published by Rivershore Books & available in
E-book & printed versions.

RANDOM THOUGHTS OF A STUPID MAN

MORE RANDOM THOUGHTS OF A STUPID MAN

STILL A STUPID MAN

A GUIDE TO MIDDLE SCHOOL & BEYOND

I STILL OWN A FLIP PHONE

Available in e-books and printed versions.

Available at:

www.rivershorebooks.com
www.amazon.com
www.barnesandnoble.com
www.nookpress.com
www.smashwords.com
Piragasis' Northwoods Store: Ely, MN
Mitchell-Tappan House Bed and Breakfast: Hibbing, MN

RIVERSHORE BOOKS

www.rivershorebooks.com
info@rivershorebooks.com
www.facebook.com/rivershore.books
www.twitter.com/rivershorebooks
blog.rivershorebooks.com
forum.rivershorebooks.com

www.ingramcontent.com/pod-product-compliance
Lightning Source LLC
Chambersburg PA
CBHW071556040426
42452CB00008B/1188